Strippers

A play

Peter Terson

Samuel French - London
New York - Sydney - Toronto - Hollywood

STRIPPERS

Strippers was first presented by the TyneWear Theatre Company at the Newcastle Playhouse on 6th March, 1984, with the following cast:

Cilla	Pamela Blackwood
Wendy	Judi Lamb
Aunt Ada	Lyn Douglas
Bernard	Brendan Healey
Dougie	Sammy Johnson
Harry	Alan Hockey
Michelle	Tracie Elizabeth Gillman
Paulie	Shaun Prendergast
Buffy	Susannah Fellows

Directed by John Blackmore
Designed by Robert Jones

The play was subsequently presented at the Phoenix Theatre, London by Duncan C. Weldon with Paul Gregg and Lionel Becker for Triumph Apollo Productions Ltd, and Jerome Minskoff, on 29th May, 1985, with the following cast:

Cilla	Pamela Blackwood
Wendy	Judi Lamb
Aunt Ada	Lyn Douglas
Bernard	Brendan Healy
Dougie	Rod Culbertson
Harry	Bill Maynard
Michelle	Jackie Lye
Paulie	Gavin Muir
Buffy	Lynda Bellingham
Barmaid	Denise Bryson

The play directed by John Blackmore
Designed by Saul Radomsky

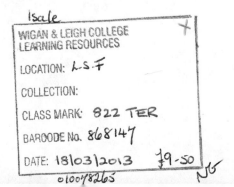

SYNOPSIS OF SCENES

Act I
  Scene 1   The Club—concert room and lounge
  Scene 2   The café
  Scene 3   Bernard's house
  Scene 4   Harry's office
  Scene 5   A bare room
  Scene 6   Bernard's house
  Scene 7   The dressing-room
  Scene 8   The stage of the Excelsior Club

Act II
  Scene 1   Bernard's house
  Scene 2   Outside the C.I.U. Club
  Scene 3   Buffy's flat
  Scene 4   Wendy's and Bernard's bedroom
  Scene 5   The Club—concert room and lounge
  Scene 6   Bernard's house—the kitchen
  Scene 7   A pub
  Scene 8   A stage

Time: the present

CHARACTERS

Cilla, a stripper
Wendy Robson, a Walker housewife
Aunt Ada, Bernard's aunt
Bernard Robson, Wendy's husband
Dougie, Bernard's mate
Harry, the strippers' agent
Paulie, Harry's nephew and secretary
Michelle, a stripper
Buffy, a stripper
Barmaid

ACT I*

SCENE 1

The Club—Concert Room

The Lights come up on a shimmery curtain as the voice of the Club Secretary is heard

Club Secretary (*off*) Gentlemen, members, lads, settle down for the first stripper of the show ... If you'll take your hands out of your pockets, where they don't belong, and put them together to welcome, a return visit of that great performer, the scintillating CILLA.

Cilla enters. The play starts with a strip act proper
Cilla's Act
At the end of the strip, the shimmery curtain parts to reveal ...

The Club Lounge

Wendy is sitting alone at a table. The Barmaid is behind the bar

Aunt Ada enters

Wendy (*to the Barmaid*) Vodka and orange and a half of shandy please — ta.
Ada Hello pet.
Wendy Hello Aunt Ada.
Ada Where is he?
Wendy In the Concert Room.
Ada What's up there?
Wendy The Exotic Dancers.
Ada The strippers?
Wendy Yes.
Ada Do him good. Take his mind off things.
Wendy I suppose it will, won't it?
Ada I don't know what they see in it. I once saw a male stripper, he did nowt for me.
Wendy I think they're more of a joke meself.
Ada He's taking it bad, isn't he? Being made redundant. The whole yard closing down. Eeeh, I never expected that. I was hoping for a last-minute reprieve. There was talk of Nissan those Japanese taking it over at the last minute, but no. I suppose they're probably too busy buying up Sunderland.
Wendy It's his trade being made obsolete that upsets him most.

---

*NB. Paragraph 3 on page ii of this Acting Edition regarding photo-copying and video-recording should be carefully read.

Ada Ay, funny thing that, he seems to come from an obsolete line. His Uncle Benny was the last of the Angle Iron smiths in Swan Hunters, you know. It's a trade you never hear of now, like pattern-maker, there's another one ... still, I suppose that's progress, new methods taking over.

Wendy And what's he supposed to do? Sit in the Club for the rest of his life?

Ada He'll do something, never fear. He's a trier. The Robson men are all triers. His Uncle Stan was rejected by eight police forces because of his height, standards were very stringent in those days ... but he tried and kept on trying.

Wendy Did he get one?

Ada Eventually, yes, Hong Kong ... but it didn't agree with him. It was all knives in the back ...

Bernard enters

Wendy Hello pet.

Ada Hello son, did you enjoy it?

Bernard Ay, it was all right.

Ada I don't know what you see in it myself. Not that I've seen it, I couldn't be bothered. Well, your Great Aunt Bella was the midwife for Low Walker so I suppose I inherited it from her.

Bernard Inherited what?

Ada No interest.

Dougie enters

Dougie Did you see the stripper, Bernard? (*To the Barmaid*) Pint of Fed please, mate. That little one went like a whippet didn't she? She'd have made a good jockey. There's another spot later on ye knaa. I saw her come in. She moves like the Lampton Worm, great big goggly eyes...

Bernard Oh man Dougie boy, don't talk about strippers in front of the women.

Dougie I'm sorry about that, was I speaking out of turn?

Wendy You want to watch your Social Graces, Dougie man.

Dougie Ay, sorry.

Ada It's all right son. Can you not take him away for a bit of healthy exercise?

Dougie I've got wor name down on the snooker table. Howway Bernard.

Dougie goes

Ada Ay, off you go son.

Wendy Ay, go on. You've got my approval as well.

Bernard goes

Ada It won't do to let him mope y'know.

Wendy No.

Ada There's others been paid off before him and there's others will again.

Wendy That helps I must say, Aunt Ada.

Ada Is there nothing else he can do?

Wendy Not that I've noticed.
Ada Can you not get him anything?
Wendy Me?
Ada In your line.
Wendy My line?
Ada You meet people.
Wendy Aunt Ada, man, you seem to have a very grand idea of what a part-time market researcher is.
Ada It gets you out.
Wendy Not in the Corridors of Power...
Ada You went to Ponteland that time.
Wendy To cover the cattle show for Spillers.
Ada Will you keep it up?
Wendy I'll have to look for something more if Bernard gets nothing.
Ada You might get a vacancy at our place. I could put in a good word for you.
Wendy Washing dishes.
Ada No, you're too good for that, waitressing—there's sometimes vacancies. You can work shifts to give you time to look after the bairn.
Wendy I'll have to think of something.
Ada Waitressing is all right. If you can stand the running about involved.
Wendy I might need your legs.
Ada You can have them and all if it'll do you any good. I'm going to get a bingo card, do you want one?
Wendy Not the night.
Ada I'll go alone then. Hi, *you're* not getting morbid are you?
Wendy No Aunt Ada.
Ada Good. Enough with one, it wouldn't do for two in the family ... runs in the Robsons ... his Uncle Jim dropped off the end of the Naval Yard crane you know ... they say it was an accident but I'll swear to this day the bugger jumped. He was a long-faced so-and-so that one...
Wendy It didn't come out in you Aunt Ada...
Ada No, I take after my mother's side ... it was my father's side that were all twisty-faced. But they came from Wallsend anyway.

She goes

Cilla enters with Harry

Harry (*speaking to off*) Don't ever call that "an appearance". Did you see her! (*To the Barmaid*) Give us a large brandy pet. She begged me for the second spot and gave them that. They were expecting a stripper, not a clown.
Cilla She wasn't all that bad, was she Harry? She's pretty enough, you'll give her that surely?
Harry Pretty ... I don't run a model agency, I run *strippers* ...
Cilla She's not frightened to come down off the stage, you'll give 'er that.
Harry Oh no, she'll come down off the stage all right. I sometimes wish she didn't. (*He sits*) That was the Concert Secretary's ale she knocked

over ... and when she sat on the table and got up she had a beer mat stuck to her arse ... when she got back on the stage she looked like a one-eyed feller with his teeth out.

Cilla Give her a chance Harry, she's inventive.

Harry Inventive ... she's got me guessing.

Michelle enters

Michelle How was I, Harry?

Harry Nerve bending.

Michelle Did you like my routine?

Harry I think you can dispense with that feather duster.

Michelle Why? I'm supposed to be a chambermaid.

Harry You just used it to dust the furniture! If you're going to have a feather duster, do something sensible with it. Howway, drink up ... have you got transport?

Cilla I'm being picked up.

Michelle I need a ride Harry ...

Harry Do yer.

Michelle Uhuh.

Harry Oh ay, come on then.

Michelle Which way are you going?

Harry Well, not through the Tyne Tunnel with you—the bugger'd cave in.

Dougie and Bernard enter

Dougie If those buggers don't pot black soon it'll change colour with age.

Bernard They're frightened of it, man.

Wendy What happened to the snooker?

Dougie We were pipped.

Bernard There's another name up ahead of me.

Dougie Committee man, he'll be on all night, they play to the rules you see.

Wendy Does that mean I get the honour of your company for a while then?

Dougie Forever if those buggers don't get a move on. Hi, do you want to play pool?

Bernard No, it cramps my style.

Dougie Dominoes then?

Bernard I'm not in a dominoes mood the night.

Dougie Darts? Cards, owt?

Bernard No, not for me ...

Dougie What'll we do till the table's clear ...?

Wendy You might be forced to sit and talk to me.

Dougie We don't want to keep you from yer bingo.

Wendy Thanks for the consideration.

Dougie Hi, hang on, is that one of the strippers?

Wendy How do you expect me to know.

Dougie Bernard, would you recognize her? We saw most of her the other way up.

Bernard It's her all right.
Dougie Drinking in the lounge as well.
Wendy She's been in for some time.
Dougie Should we ask her to take her pants off and say "hello" to an old friend?
Wendy Dougie man, shurrup.
Bernard Have you been talking to her?
Wendy What do you take me for?
Dougie I'll talk to her ... Hi darling, good show that.
Cilla Thanks.
Dougie Doing owt the night?
Cilla Yes, I'm taken care of thanks.
Dougie I bet she bloody is an all.

Paulie enters

Paulie Ready?
Cilla I'll just finish me drink.
Paulie You're on at the Excelsior at half-past ...
Cilla We'll get to the Excelsior ...
Dougie You can see the rings on that bugger's fingers. He can hardly get his fag up to his mouth.
Bernard I bet they're not for show either.
Dougie I wouldn't like a knuckle sandwich off him that bugger.
Cilla (*to Paulie*) Away then.
Dougie Good-night darling ...

Paulie and Cilla go

Bernard He must be her bloke ...
Dougie Pimp man, bloody pimp. She cannot have an ordinary bloke doing a job like that.
Bernard Whoever he is he sees a lot of her ...
Dougie We all do, don't we.
Wendy It must be funny to have a girlfriend who you lot have seen naked.
Dougie We've more than seen her naked. Ooh I was that close I was nearly registered a missing person. It ought to be stopped man, when they on next I hope?
Wendy Does it not mean anything more to you than that?
Dougie What's she talking about?
Wendy Well, I'll try and explain should I? You go up in that concert room, twice a week and Sunday lunchtime. The girls strip in front of you. A ritual. There must be something there ... I mean, you've made contact.
Dougie I wish we bloody had.
Wendy What I'm trying to say is ...
Bernard You don't know what you're trying to say, that's your trouble.
Wendy Well I'm trying ... what I'm saying is ... there must be some sort of relationship between you and her.
Dougie Us and *it* ...

Wendy Oh, forget it . . .

She goes

Dougie What was she talking about?
Bernard I think she's upset because I was made redundant.
Dougie Oh ay. Bound to be ... it makes them inarticulate a bit of
worry ... Mind she had me stumped for words meself for a minute. I
mean ye cannot just tell her ye gan up to see a bit of fanny. Howway
let's see if that table's clear.

They exit

Black-out

SCENE 2

The Café

Wendy is wiping the tables. Buffy is sitting at a table

Wendy Can I help you?
Buffy Sure ... say, you're new here?
Wendy Yes.
Buffy What happened to old Alice? Varicose veins pack up?
Wendy They didn't tell me that ... just said there was a vacancy.
Buffy A vacancy here usually means a coffin ... Don't let me put you off
a startling career. Three coffees.
Wendy Three?
Buffy I've got pals coming ... oh and two chocolate biscuits, let's see a
fight against temptation. Hi, aren't those heels a little high for this job?
Old Alice worked in carpet slippers.
Wendy Old Alice smoked Weights as well. I don't. (*During the following,
she pours three coffees and takes them and two biscuits to Buffy's table*)
Buffy Smart girl.

Michelle enters

Hi honey. Paid your dues? What a way to start the week eh? Monday
morning and Harry pawing over the hard-earned greenbacks ...
Michelle Ay, why it's worth it just to see him pleasant.
Buffy As pleasant as an avaricious frog can be ... Still, he'll be able to get
his wanking machine serviced ... Note the new waitress. Is she, or is she
not an improvement on old Alice? I'm only asking.
Michelle Let's see how much coffee she's spilled in the saucer ...
Both A definite improvement ...
Michelle Two chocolate biscuits. Oh, Buffy man, you know I'm slimming.
Buffy Sure, leave it then ... Cilla can have two ... amazing how much
that girl can put away ... and still keep her figure.

Michelle Oh I can as well, but I'm just practising control.
Buffy Good on yer babe.
Michelle Have you had one?
Buffy Me. Dozens ...
Michelle Shall I weaken? Just this once?
Buffy I won't think any the less of you. But you know you've just demonstrated that lack of resolve which is the basic root of our profession ...
Michelle You make us feel rotten now.
Buffy Well, a little moral training doesn't come amiss on a Monday morning. Now, why were you so long with our beloved Dirty Harry?
Michelle He had words to say about my chambermaid act ...
Buffy He would, he's allergic to feather dusters ...
Michelle I thought it was a good prop, Buffy, but he just doesn't like it ...
Buffy Aw, chuck something else at him ...
Michelle I am, I am. I've got this new sailor boy routine worked out, with a lot of flags.
Buffy (*singing*) "Join the navy, and see the seven seas, In the navy ..."
Michelle That's right. How did you guess?
Buffy Intuition my dear, pure intuition ...

Paulie enters

Paulie Ah, Michelle ...
Michelle Hello Paulie.
Paulie Morning Buffy ...

Buffy ignores him

Morning Buffy.
Buffy I've seen you once already this morning, what the hell do you want? A reception?
Paulie Michelle, I was talking to Uncle Harry about your thoughts for a new act.
Michelle Oh, were you.
Paulie They sound very interesting. Original ... will you join me for a minute and we'll have a word? Just when you've finished your coffee.
Michelle Thanks very much Paulie ... where shall we meet?
Paulie In the big back room, in case you want to run through anything ...
Michelle I haven't got anything with me Paulie.
Paulie We'll just have words then ...

He goes

Buffy That guy always puts a skin on my coffee ... Listen kid, he reaches out to all the new girls, nice as ninepence, and puts the screws on them ... into bed or they find their engagements cut down.
Michelle Oh God ... I don't want my engagements cut down.
Buffy It's what's called the baptism of nausea ... but if you grit your teeth and hang on you'll pull though ... if your act is good, you'll get bookings ... if not—it's beddings.

Cilla enters

Cilla Hiya! Once Dirty Harry takes his whack there's bugger all left. Is that my coffee?

Buffy It was Samantha's but she hasn't arrived yet ...

Cilla She won't, she dashed off for a driving lesson.

Buffy Has traffic control been alerted?

Cilla Can I cut my way through this coffee then?

Buffy Sure, help yourself ... Where were you Saturday night?

Cilla Byker and Heaton Social Club.

Michelle I want to go there, to gain experience ...

Buffy What a place for the inexperienced ...

Cilla At the moment pet I think you still need SPACE ... Has Paulie been in?

Michelle ⎫ (*together*) ⎫ Aye ... *etc.*
Buffy ⎭   ⎬ (*drowning her voice*) just passed ... like a spectre ...
                      ⎭ he turned the silver paper on the biscuit rusty ...

Cilla Did he ask for me?

Michelle ⎫ (*together*) ⎫ No he ...
Buffy ⎭   ⎬ I think he's expecting you in the back room ... finish
                      ⎭ your coffee ...

Wendy Can I clear away now?

Buffy Hi, don't look too eager. They crucify people for less than that. Sit down, rest the pins and tell us of the outside world.

Wendy I don't think that's encouraged ...

Buffy We're regulars here, Monday mornings. A girl's legs were not made to be stood on ... shall I rephrase that?

Wendy No, it's all right. I'm used to standing, I do market research, and demonstrating.

Cilla Do yer? What do you demonstrate?

Wendy Anything that comes up ... there are all sorts of products, some of them are quite nice ... we get samples sometimes ...

Buffy So you do this job, *and* demonstrate?

Wendy Worse luck. What do you do?

Cilla We can earn in eight minutes what you do in a day in this dump.

Buffy In other dumps of course ...

Wendy But what do you do?

Michelle We're billed as "Exotic Dancers" ...

Buffy In reality we just get 'em off, show 'em our fannies and run.

Cilla We're strippers.

Wendy Oh. Ay.

Buffy Don't run away ...

Wendy I'm not ... where do you do it?

Cilla We do the clubs.

Michelle Working Men's Clubs.

Buffy Wanking men's clubs.

Wendy My husband is a member of the Walker West ...

Cilla I played there last week.

Wendy I thought I knew your face.

Buffy You've been cheating.

Wendy No. No. I didn't see her act ... I saw her in the lounge.

Buffy Allowed in? What was it? Open night for the ethnic minorities?

Michelle I always find them very friendly, they always ask us over to the pool table.

Buffy How was such an innocent planted on this earth?

Harry enters

Harry I thought I'd find you lot in here. (*To Michelle*) I hope you go steady on the biscuits—they'll go straight to your ankles. (*To Wendy*) Are you the new girl?

Wendy Yes.

Harry Well you should be in my office.

Wendy I'm sorry, I don't know what you're talking about.

Harry Aren't you the ex-nurse?

Buffy She's the new waitress, Harry.

Harry New waitress? Oh I'll have a coffee.

Wendy White?

Harry Ay, with milk ... I thought she was the new lass. I got a very promising phone call ... trained nurse ... cannot get a job ... sounded perfect ... hasn't turned up though.

Buffy Why don't you complain to the BMA?

Michelle You'll just have to keep on relying on us, Harry.

Harry God help us, I've got no alternative ... (*Taking the coffee from Wendy*) Ta.

Michelle She moves well, Harry.

Harry Ay, for a waitress.

Buffy She's got a certain style about her ...

Michelle She could do a waitress act ...

Buffy Nice long legs, what do you think, Cilla?

Cilla She's got all the moves but she's got nowt else.

Wendy Excuse me, who do you think you're looking at?

Buffy Just admiring your style, girl.

Wendy Thanks very much, but this isn't the Appleby Horse Show ...

Buffy Nice turn of phrase too.

Michelle Is your hair natural?

Wendy Look, I'm here to serve coffee not to be studied at from every angle ...

Buffy If you're real nice to him this gentleman might offer you a job.

Wendy Have you got cafés?

Harry Cafés? It takes me all my time to run a coffee machine ...

Buffy Singing the same old song.

Cilla Hard done by, isn't he?

Harry If you think I get rich keeping you lot in work ...

Buffy The last of the great providers ...

Wendy What sort of job are you thinking of?

Harry I employ Exotic Dancers.

Wendy Stripper, you gotta be joking . . .

Harry Hi, before you get high-handed, don't abuse a profession before
the practitioners.

Wendy I'm sorry, I didn't mean to, but I'm married and got a bairn . . .

Buffy So what, lots of our girls are married.

Wendy Are they?

Michelle And they've got bairns as well.

Wendy But I thought . . .

Harry Thought what?

Wendy I just thought . . .

Harry You're like a lot of other people, you thought you knew something
you know bugger all about. You've got the wrong impression. These
girls are members of the acting profession. If you want to give it a try
I'll see you, if not, keep on serving tea and stotty cakes and keep your
ideas to yourself. I'd better go and see if that nurse has turned up. By
the time she arrives I shall bloody well need her.

He goes

Michelle Nice to hear Harry on his high horse, eh?

Wendy Have I upset him?

Buffy You touched him on his point of morality . . . the dignity of his
professional status . . .

Wendy Did he mean what he said, y'know about seeing us?

Cilla He'll see you all right, but that doesn't mean anything, you might
have all the moves but it takes more than that . . .

Wendy What else does it take?

Cilla Personality for a start . . . I'm gonna go and drop in on Paulie . . .

She goes

Wendy Have I upset her an' all?

Buffy She's frightened of all newcomers, basic sense of insecurity.

Wendy Well you can tell her I'm not a newcomer, I couldn't do that
anyway.

Buffy Course you could. You can walk, you can wait on tables, baby,
that's basically what we do.

Michelle To musical variations.

Buffy The tables are laden with booze, instead of coffee.

Michelle And the walk is . . . so so exaggerated . . .

Buffy But it ain't eight hours a day . . .

Wendy You make taking your clothes off sound easy.

Buffy It is, there's always a demand . . .

Wendy Is it pin money?

Buffy Pin money like hell. We can earn twice what your husband brings
home in a week. You heard the guy, we're professionals . . .

Michelle There's a union.

Buffy Somewhere!

Michelle Girls *used* to do it for pin money, in the old days but the agent
doesn't like that . . . he likes to know his girls can be relied upon.

Buffy So there you are girl, it's open to you ... all you have to do now is get yourself an agent.

Wendy Agent! Oh come on—where do you find an agent round here.

Buffy There's only one agent.

Both Dirty Harry ...

Wendy No, I couldn't do it thanks ... I'd rather stick to this, at the moment ... (*She clears up*)

Buffy Yes ... there's always something to stick with *at the moment* ... just make sure the moment doesn't turn into a lifetime, doll.

Black-out

SCENE 3

Bernard's house. Evening

Bernard is sitting at the table drinking tea. There is a kitchen off

Dougie enters

Dougie Howway, man, Club's open and you're still drinking tea ...

Bernard Wendy's not back from work yet ...

Dougie You've got to get yourself better organized than this ... her not back and the Club open ...

Bernard She works a full day ...

Dougie (*picking up a note*) What the hell's this? Standing orders? (*He reads*) "Pre-heat oven at seven for fifteen minutes ... Take lasagne out of tray top of freezer, place on a baking tray, pierce foil in several places with knife, place in oven for forty minutes ... Put lettuce to soak and clean and set table ..." Have you done all this?

Bernard I'm in the middle of it ...

Dougie She's efficient your Wendy ... you'd never have thought she'd have turned into this from Miss Whitley Bay ...

Bernard Ay, they change ...

Dougie Very adaptable these women, that's why I divvent want one till I'm beyond all change meself. Well, away then are you coming?

Bernard How can I man?

Dougie Just add a PS to this note ... "Got sick of washing the lettuce, put it in the washing machine, regulo seven, gone to the Club."

Bernard Just sit down, she'll be in in a minute, man, just wait ...

Dougie Have you been down to job centre?

Bernard Ay ...

Dougie What do you expect to find? Salaried position for permanent optimist.

Bernard You've got to keep trying, man.

Dougie Oh ay, what for?

Bernard For your own self-respect.

Dougie There's no demand for self-respect. Just read the *Financial Times* and you'll see they're not employing it.

Bernard You're a bloody cynic you are ...

Dougie I might be, but I don't see ships on the Tyne when there is none ... By the time they start building ships down Swan Hunter's again they'll have a job getting somebody who remembers where the sharp end goes ... However, divvent let me dampen your spirits ... Here's your lass ... she must have been yapping at the bus stop.

Wendy enters

Wendy This house is cold ...

Bernard It shouldn't be, I've got a bar on ...

Wendy What about the central heating ...?

Bernard Oh, I thought I'd set it ...

Wendy I'll do it ... hello Dougie ... where's the bairn?

Bernard With Aunty Ada, she'll be back in a minute ...

Wendy Is there a cup of tea in that pot?

Bernard It needs cheering up a bit ...

Wendy I'll do it ...

She goes off to the kitchen with the teapot

Dougie She comes through like a dose of salts. Duty Officer's inspection of the Household Cavalry.

Wendy (*off*) Do you call that salad prepared?

Bernard I've washed the lettuce.

Wendy enters

Wendy You haven't man, you've just left it soaking in the sink. How long's the lasagne been in?

Bernard I've just put it in ...

Wendy Did you pre-heat the oven ...?

Bernard Ay, just for a minute, it was eating up electricity ...

Wendy That's a false economy, Bernard man.

Bernard So am I by the looks of things ...

Wendy Get the table set then ...

She goes out

Bernard Bollocks.

Dougie Get the table set man.

Bernard Bugger this for a lark ... (*He gets a tablecloth, cutlery etc. from the sideboard*)

Dougie Throw the cloth on man, keep her face straight. Here man, I'll give you a hand if it'll make you feel any better ... it's like putting the ground sheet down. Can you remember camping up Ovingham ... when we were Cubs.

Bernard Ay ... in that second-hand American Army tent ...

Dougie Lightweight camping, yon bugger it weighted a ton.

Bernard On wor bikes ...

Dougie Sand-shoes and football shorts, didn't we fancy worselves eh?

Bernard Davy Crockett and his mate ...
Dougie Still, we used to get them Ovingham lasses.
Bernard I did! They used to come out of curiosity to look at you and ended up on the grass with me!
Dougie Ended up in the bracken with me, mate!
Bernard Did they bugger, like hell? Good times eh?
Dougie Great times. All too short man, all too short.
Bernard Great times. Pity they're over.
Dougie Speak for yourself man ...

Wendy enters

There we are pet, all spread out, fit for a picnic.
Wendy What are all those dishes on the draining-board?
Bernard Oh, they're nowt ...
Wendy And towels all over the place ... I don't want to come back and find the house worse than I left it ...
Bernard Well Aunt Ada said she would ...
Wendy Don't leave everything to your Aunt Ada ... I left *you* in charge, not Aunt Ada ...
Bernard I'm not a bloody skivvy ...
Wendy Oh but I am, am I? ... and where are you going?
Bernard The Club ...
Wendy You're not, Bernard ...
Bernard I'm going to the Club ...
Dougie You're not Bernard, but I am ...

Dougie goes

Bernard I'll be along in a minute.
Wendy You won't, Bernard.
Bernard Don't tell me what I will and won't do.
Wendy I left a note for you this morning before you were up and about, I don't want to come back to a cold and empty house ...
Bernard What shall I do eh? Light the candles and open a bottle of champagne?
Wendy A good idea Bernard ... yes, let's try and maintain a few standards, light the candles, and finish laying the table, for two ...
Bernard I'm going out ...
Wendy On no Bernard, I've been on my feet all day and I want a home to come back to.
Bernard What the hell do you think I've been doing all day? I've been up to the town, looking for work, looking at non-existent bloody job vacancies till I'm sick.
Wendy All right, and I've been working for the money, I'll expect you to do your share at home ...
Bernard If you don't like it, don't do it.
Wendy And what'll I do, eh, walk the streets?
Bernard I don't care what you do, just don't come complaining to me when you've had enough of it.

Wendy Well I've had enough of this.
Bernard Is this all the gratitude I get for a life of working my fingers to the bone ...?
Wendy I stood by you when you were working, try standing by me will you?
Bernard What the hell do you want? Medals?
Wendy All right, go to your Club, go and dip your face in a pint, sup up and forget, wait for your Giro with the rest of the lads, that's the form isn't it? Well it might suit you, but it doesn't suit me.
Bernard Well you better bloody well find something that *does* suit you.
Wendy I will, Bernard, I will ...
Bernard Good, keep us posted ...
Wendy Wait Bernard. I know it must be humiliating for you, but don't let it come between us ... we've got a bairn, we've got each other. We'll manage.
Bernard Ay, all right.

He goes

Wendy gets out a business card ...

Black-out

SCENE 4

Harry's Office. Day

Harry is sitting with Paulie

Harry Marianne, twelve-fifteen South Shield Legion. Twelve-thirty-five, the Tunnel Club.
Paulie Can't be done, can't be done.
Harry What do you mean? "Can't be done." It's twenty minutes between engagements, she can do that if the taxi driver gets his foot down.
Paulie She's played the Tunnel Club twice this month ...
Harry Well? So what.
Paulie It doesn't need pointing out does it?
Harry It needs *spelling* out for me man ...
Paulie They're sick of her.
Harry Well they'll be even then, 'cos she must be sick of them.
Paulie Howway Harry, see sense ...
Harry What's all this Harry business, it's *Uncle* Harry if you're complaining.
Paulie Try Phyllis, she's fresh.
Harry Phyllis doesn't do South Shields and district, her family belong there.
Paulie Try Marguerite then.
Harry She's doing the Ashington Leek Show, by special demand. And

divvent ask what the connection is between the Leeks and Marguerite, I've never been able to work it out mesel'.

Paulie Annabelle then.

Harry Annabelle is out of commission for a week; besides they're not struck on coloured down there ...

Paulie Miranda ...

Harry Oh bloody Miranda, Marguerite, Annabelle, Phyllis. I shall go round the twist. I'm going to put myself in a coffin with this job. Eighty-three girls on my books and two hundred clubs to provide for ... I need a bloody computer.

Paulie Get one then.

Harry What would I do with you?

Paulie Oh man Harry.

Harry Oh, this bloody hair is too tight—here, come and loosen it will you, from the back ... don't pull it, it cost a fortune ... careful ... mind the gauze.

There is a knock at the door

Wait a minute! Put it back! Come in.

Buffy enters

Oh it's you.

Buffy Can I come into the Think Tank?

Harry It looks as if you're already in.

Buffy I'd like to introduce my new protégé.

Paulie Is this the new lass you were telling us about?

Buffy Sure, but she's no good to you, Paulie, she's borne a child.

Harry What the hell's she talking about?

Buffy Just a little joke between Paulie and me.

Harry It better be a joke as well or I'll have the pair of you on your arse ... Howway and fetch her in ... what's her name?

Buffy Wendy ... you may enter the shrine Wendy ... don't be shy, they're housetrained ... just.

Wendy enters

Harry Is that any way to introduce a prospective employee? Get her a chair, you grinning bugger. Oy! Paul, don't sod about. We meet again. So you've changed your mind eh, you want to be a stripper.

Wendy I'd like to try it.

Harry It's not a matter of *trying* it, it's a matter of *doing* it. I've got enough triers around here, believe me.

Paulie Are you going to stick to it, apply yourself for a long period of time?

Wendy Yes, I think so.

Harry Don't *think* so, *know* so ...

Buffy Think positive, pet.

Wendy Yes, I'll stick it.

Harry Good, at least we've got that sorted out. Have you seen the other girls working?
Wendy Yes.
Harry So you know what's involved?
Wendy Yes.
Harry Who have you seen?
Wendy Cilla, Gillian, Buffy ... Michelle ...
Harry Michelle, Christ, don't take a leaf out of her book or we'll all be in trouble. Well, all right then, if you know exactly what it's all about ...
Paulie One question.
Harry I thought there might be.
Paulie What are you doing it for?
Harry Ay, good point son. That's very important as far as we're concerned. You're not doing it for *pin* money are you? Or holiday money, or clothes allowance.
Wendy No. My husband's unemployed, and we've gorra bairn.
Harry Now that's good. No chance of him getting a job in the near future I take it?
Wendy Not in his trade.
Harry Good, good.
Paulie What's his trade?
Wendy Centre lathe turner.
Paulie Ah well there's not much demand for them now ...
Harry Good, good, it's always good if the husband is relying on the wife's income.
Buffy With any luck he'll hang himself.
Paulie That's enough from you.
Buffy Go find a web and make a home.
Harry Hi, this happens to be my office, not a backyard, let's have a bit of decorum. Sorry about that, love ... now, you said you had a bairn Wendy, er ... have you got any stretch marks?
Buffy Not as many as *you*, Harry.
Harry I wasn't asking you.
Buffy Keep your hair on.
Harry And I've warned you about remarks like that. Well, Wendy, have you?
Wendy What?
Harry Stretch marks.
Wendy No, I haven't.
Harry And you can dance I take it?
Wendy Yes.
Harry And you live in ... ?
Wendy Walker.
Harry Nice area Walker, it'll be lovely once it's finished. So, you wouldn't be averse to playing South Shields this Sunday.
Wendy Sunday?
Harry You're not a Catholic are you?
Wendy No.

Harry Thank Christ for that, Sunday is our busiest time ... it's this weekend then.

Wendy But I haven't done it before!

Harry Well it's only Tuesday. Buffy, can you train her up? Get her an act together for Sunday?

Buffy Sure, no problem.

Paulie And I'll be in and out to see how you're going along.

Buffy Bring a basin with you and we can all be sick.

Harry What the hell's got into you two? I was under the erroneous impression I had a happy and harmonious staff, not a warring faction.

Paulie Shall we bury the hatchet?

Buffy Sure, where do you want it?

Harry That's it! Enough of the double act! Sorry about that Wendy. Before you go—this is all right with your husband I take it?

Wendy I haven't told him yet ... I thought I'd wait till after my first engagement.

Paulie (*whispering*) Friday.

Harry Yes. I think you're right ... In that case, better make it Friday night at the Denton Excelsior.

Wendy Friday!

Harry Night. It's very quiet. But after that I want it all in the open. That's all then ... I'll be in Thursday to see how you're getting on with your act ... get her a contract.

Wendy What if it's no good?

Harry You'll be all right, Buffy'll sort you out. Remember, (*reading out the notice pinned to the wall*) "No Obscenity, No Double Acts, No Private Arrangements." And no cheques, cash only.

Paulie (*getting out a contract*) Sign here.

Harry Read it on the way home.

Paulie A copy for you.

Buffy C'mon kid, now you've glimpsed the big time, let's get a breath of fresh air.

They go

Paulie I was wondering ... should we be cutting down on Buffy's engagements?

Harry Cutting down? I've got full order books and you talk about cutting down?

Paulie Only wondering.

Harry Ay, well, wonder to yourself.

Paulie She hasn't done Scotswood Road Non-Political Club for a long time.

Harry By Christ, you really must hate her. No. I'm not having any victimization in my agency. She can go there on *Sunday.*

Black-out

SCENE 5

A bare room. Morning

There is one chair at the back

Michelle and Cilla enter

Michelle Nobody here yet ... oh lush, the heat's on ... (*She fiddles with her tape recorder*) I'll just rewind.
Cilla What have you got for us to hear this time?
Michelle To *see* ... to *see* ... I have a brand new act to show.
Cilla Are you going to show us then or is it still in mothballs?
Michelle Wait and see ... I'll give you a clue, can you guess from this? (*She switches on the tape recorder; it plays a spurt of terrible discord*) Ah! it's gone ...
Cilla You're not very strong on the technical side are you?
Michelle Not really. I need a man to look after me ...
Cilla You better look for a sound engineer ... let's have a look.

Buffy and Wendy enter

Buffy Morning chickens.
Michelle Buffy, I have a new act to show you.
Buffy Why not? Always ready for one of your imaginative leaps, kid.
Cilla I thought you were training Wendy?
Buffy So we are.
Cilla We? I'm not giving away any of my tips.
Buffy It's a good thing you're a stripper, Cilla, you part with nowt else ... OK Michelle, Wendy hasn't got her costume together yet, so why don't you give her a little demonstration.
Michelle Demonstrate? Can I demonstrate?
Buffy You do it all the time.
Michelle Eh?
Buffy To it, get changed ...
Michelle Lush!

Michelle dashes off

Buffy Now Wendy, you've brought some music?
Wendy I've got a few bits that I thought might appeal.
Buffy Basically what you need is two four-minute tracks, so you make yourself a tape eight minutes long.
Wendy Is that all?
Buffy Baby, any more and those guys would be coming in their pants ... now the thing you've got to watch is the transition from one track to the other ... there's nothing worse than standing up there wriggling your ass and waiting for the record to change.
Cilla Do you know any good sound engineers?
Wendy No.
Cilla Do you know any electricians?

Wendy No.
Cilla Who do you know?
Buffy I can get it taped for you, there's a really good ...
Cilla Oh yeah, you know everybody don't you?
Buffy Aren't I the lucky girl! The main thing to watch, when you get your costume, is not to get all of it off before the first four minutes ... otherwise you're doing a health and efficiency routine for the next four ...OK let's see what you got. Hi, did you buy a *new* tape recorder?
Wendy Yes.
Buffy What *brand new*?
Wendy Yes—on credit.
Buffy How do you hope to recoup at seventeen pounds a spot? In this game, girl, you invest in the minimum ...
Cilla Oh no look, it's best to have good sound recorded at the beginning.
Buffy Yeah, maybe, but when you see the sound equipment some of the clubs have, all you can do is hand your tape to the Entertainment Secretary and hope for the best ... However, if you've expended, you've expended ...
Cilla Anyway you can always get rid of a good second-hand one if you don't come up to scratch ...
Wendy Shall I dance?

Wendy switches on the tape recorder and dances

Buffy Wendy, turn it off for a sec.
Wendy (*turning the music off*) Well, what do you think?
Cilla I'll be honest, if I'm allowed ...
Wendy Please do.
Cilla I don't think it'll grab them, it's got no balls.
Buffy Yeah, its rhythms are too subtle. These boys really pride themselves on their primitive beat. Next ...

Wendy switches on the tape recorder. Music, Wendy dances

Stop, one of the other girls has been using that in her routine for weeks ...

Wendy switches off the tape

Cilla And you cannot copy, it's no good ... you cannot copy.
Wendy OK. I got this one off the radio—this might do. (*She switches on the music*)
Buffy No ... sorry ... too slow a start honey ... when you come on the music has to grab them ...
Wendy (*winding the tape on*) Oh, this'll grab 'em ... (*She switches on another piece of music*)
Buffy No, not that ... that's died a death and so will you.
Wendy (*switching off*) That's the lot I'm afraid.
Cilla Not very bright was it?
Buffy Don't worry, don't be discouraged, it's not easy to find the right

music. The thing about your music, right, listen to your Aunty Buffy
... it's either got to be an *ascending newie* ... ok ... or a perennial old
favourite, like the Rolling Stones or Buddy Holly ... or a piece of
familiar foreignish *exotica*. These guys in the audience have few senses
left but hearing is one of them ... See what you think of these. (*She
takes a tape from her bag and puts it in the tape recorder.*
Cilla And if I can give you a bit of advice ...
Buffy Had a change of heart, Cilla?
Cilla Be more aware ... you're thinking of yourself too much ... think
outwards ... not inwards.
Buffy Good point ... for Christ's sake don't get carried away or you'll be
giving it away.
Cilla You're a performer ... so perform ...
Buffy See if this stirs your juices. (*She switches on the tape*)

Wendy dances, starts to look good

Great. (*She switches off*) Now, how did that grab you?
Wendy Fine, I liked it.
Cilla It suited you.
Buffy That's one decided on then ... what we need is another track to give
you your full eight minutes ...
Wendy Do you ever do an encore?
Buffy What the hell you going to give them? Gymnastics?
Cilla It's gather up your clothes and get off quick ...
Buffy You just give them your act ... then byeee ...
Wendy But I haven't got an act yet ...
Buffy Let's get your music sorted out first ... How does this grab you?
(*She switches on the tape recorder*)
Wendy No, it's the Stones—I can't stand them!
Cilla Good, she's getting choosey.
Wendy Is that all right? To be choosey.
Buffy You've got to get it right baby, your tape and costume is all there
is between you and the Newcastle United Fanny Club. Try this one, it's
a little slower. See what you think of this. It's nice to have a slow one.
(*She switches on the tape*)

Wendy dances again

(*Switching off*) That's it ... you got it ...
Cilla A bit big boned for me but it suits your movements all right.
Wendy It felt quite good.
Buffy By Friday you'll feel great, or like the Corporation Dustcart ...
Wendy Friday, so soon.
Cilla It pays. It doesn't give you time to get nervous ... I was ditched
straight into it overnight ...
Wendy Why was that?
Cilla Me dad threw us out of the house so to spite him I went on at his
club ... he's never lifted his face from his beer since ...
Wendy What's the next step?

Buffy The next step is to get an act together.
Cilla You need a theme ...
Wendy A theme?
Buffy Your theme has got to get to them ... stir their imaginations.
Cilla You can't just stand up and say "I'm a nice girl and I'm going to take my clothes off". It's got to be suggestion, it's all suggestion in this game.
Buffy You need to present them with a character to feed their jaded minds. A fantasy figure ... and it helps you too, it gives you a character to hide behind up there ...
Wendy Like what?
Buffy Policewomen is very popular, but Babs does a wonderful police-woman and you couldn't be expected to do what she does with her truncheon.
Wendy Truncheon?
Cilla Oh yeah, every character needs a prop ...
Buffy It's the old phallic symbol love, you forget about it in married life, but in your act you need it, the chambermaid her feather duster, the sporting girl with her hockey stick, the leather girl her whip ...
Cilla And the housewife?
Wendy The housewife?
Cilla ⎫
Buffy ⎬ (*together*) Her cucumber ...
Buffy Standard joke in the trade ... so you see, you need to invent yourself a character ...
Cilla Or two, you don't want to bore them when you're a beginner.
Wendy It seems a problem.
Buffy Don't worry, between us we'll come up with something. Michelle is full of ideas, she comes up with something new every week ...
Cilla Spends all her money on her next costume ... not to mention the accoutrements ... never thinks of the future.
Buffy Oh and you've got to think of a stage name for yourself as well. Hey Michelle, are you ready?
Michelle (*off*) Nearly, nearly ...

Michelle hurries on, with flags

Buffy (*to Michelle*) Don't be too eager. (*To Wendy*) She's tripped on the stage so often they have a St John's Ambulance guy at the back of the hall Ready? Better give her some space.

Michelle's tape recorder is switched on. Nautical music starts. Michelle does her strip but gets tangled up with her flags

Michelle I went wrong, let's do it again ...
Buffy Hang on, hang on ... what the hell you doing with those flags?
Michelle Signalling a message.
Buffy We got it, baby.
Michelle No good is it not?
Cilla You're all blinking flags ...

Buffy Look girl, Nelson couldn't do what you're trying to do.
Michelle I tell you what, I'll just use one flag.
Buffy Try that at the Navy Club and see where it gets you.

Paulie enters

Paulie Michelle, have you finished your rehearsal?
Buffy No, she hasn't. She's got two hours left.
Paulie What's she doing? Competing in the Cowes Regatta? When you're free, Michelle, I'd like to see you about this week's engagements. Just when you're free.
Cilla Oh Paulie will you hang on a minute, I'd like a word with you.

She follows him off

Buffy Is he a creep or am I losing my sense of judgement?
Michelle Ay, well I certainly wouldn't lose my head over him.
Buffy You don't have to lose anything to him, girl ... you stick by Buffy's standards.
Michelle I know but he's always threatening now engagements are getting a bit thin ...
Buffy Look, I've glimpsed that order book ... it's like the Encyclopaedia Britannica ... that thick ...
Michelle I'd better get changed despite all that.
Wendy Thanks, Michelle.
Michelle It's all right, Wendy ... good luck on Friday in the Excelsior ... tara ... Don't worry eh? You'll be smashing.

Michelle goes

Wendy Is he a bit of a problem?
Buffy He gets to all the new girls, y'know "Gimme, or else".
Wendy I better watch myself.
Buffy You're safe.
Wendy Why, because I'm married?
Buffy No because you've had a kid ... Poor Paulie has a weakness, nothing that a set of gelding irons wouldn't cure ... He needs to fantasize that all his girls are virgins and he's the Cock of the North.
Wendy Surely the girls don't fall for that?
Buffy Honey, the follies and foibles of womanhood on display. The men who've latched on to the girls in this trade are a pageant of stunted deformity ... pimps, minders, taxi drivers, fantasists. When you open your legs it's their signal to come hurtling in with their tears or threats, their lusts and lacklustre, bribery and blackmail. But let me tell you if you're going to do this job you've got to be strong within yourself. Put *all* men between you and your act. Then if you can open your legs and look through confident then you're a stripper girl.

Black-out

SCENE 6

Bernard's house. Evening

Aunt Ada is sitting in an armchair

Dougie enters

Ada Dougie is that you?

Dougie Bernard in, Aunt Ada?

Ada Dougie, I hope you've come to take him out?

Dougie I thought we might walk down to the Club, get wor name down for the snooker.

Ada Can you not take him further afield than that?

Dougie You mean there's somewhere further afield than the Club?

Ada Can you not take him to the Metro? Down to the coast?

Dougie What the hell's he thinking about like emigrating?

Ada He's getting moody . . .

Dougie Howway, what's up?

Ada He's got me worried.

Dougie You look for trouble.

Ada He's in danger of going over. It's St Nick's beckoning him. It's his redundancy. It's making him morbid. I said "Go down to the park" but he won't. Other men have been made redundant. Had a new lease of life. Bobby Watson went to Majorca on his redundancy and it lasted three months. Course things are cheaper over there . . . it's more basic living than ours . . .

Dougie What do they live in? Caves?

Ada No, it's all villas and things. His wife didn't want to go at first, but once she got there she didn't want to come back. She's back now, with a jolt. Office cleaning . . . but she's got her castanets above the mantelpiece.

Dougie Bernard needs more than a brief respite in Majorca.

Ada Precisely, I'm open to suggestions.

Dougie The Club.

Ada The Club won't do it. Try him at the coast.

Dougie Bugger the coast, it's dead till Scottish week, then it's dangerous. Bloody dangerous. I tell you what. I'll take him on a grand tour of the Affiliated Clubs . . . Denton, Westerhope, Leamington and even distant Throckley.

Ada That'll bring him out of himself . . . he's brooding. He's combing the papers every night.

Dougie What's he combing the papers for?

Ada The columns, the small ads.

Dougie That's no good. They're not even giving cheap dogs away nowadays.

Ada Poor lad. I think he's distracted. It's this unemployment. That's what did for his grandfather. He went through the Great War, the Somme, the Dardanelles without a scratch, but the nineteen twenty-three strike did him. They were always active people the Robsons, look at me.

Dougie Ay, well settle down a minute, you'll have me dizzy.
Ada There he is now. Don't let him know we're talking about him.
Dougie What are we talking about then?
Ada I don't know, do I?

They stare at each other as ...

Bernard enters with a paper

Hello pet, you were saying, Dougie?
Dougie That's not fair ... (*Loudly*) They're talking of making the South Bank of the Tyne an amenity area ...
Ada That'll be nice for them, they need summat over there ... Would you like a cup of tea now I've stayed on, Bernard?
Dougie He's coming to the Club for a pint, man. Aren't you?
Bernard Might as well, eh?
Ada A cup of tea will settle your stomach before the beer.
Dougie You have some funny bloody ideas, Ada.
Ada I'm aware of my peculiarities. Will you have a cup of tea now I've waited?

Dougie gestures to leave

Bernard Ay, we'll have a cup of tea, eh?
Dougie Ay, all right.
Ada There's a little word you know.
Dougie Oh ay, shift ... please ...

She goes off to the kitchen

Bernard She's being a treasure.
Dougie Oh ay, it's just she takes some digging up. What do you think you're doing with that paper?
Bernard Swotting flies, Dougie, what do you think?
Dougie You're scrutinizing it like a bookie studying form.
Bernard Just looking.
Dougie What do you hope to find, your own obituary?
Bernard I'm not dead yet man, not by a long way.
Dougie You're breathing heavy enough to pretend. Howway then, who's screaming out for you in the Situations Vacant?
Bernard Nobody, but I'm not looking in Situations Vacant.
Dougie Where the hell you looking? Lost and Found?
Bernard Here. Business Opportunities.
Dougie Business Bloody Opportunities.
Bernard It's about time I stood up for myself, Dougie. The only way to make money and maintain your self-respect is to go self-employed ...
Dougie Howway then, where are all these golden opportunities?
Bernard They're all over the place ... look at the top: "Mobile Kitchen, consisting of a fifteen-foot caravan, an Addas tea urn and a hot dog heater ..."
Dougie They'll have to tow it off Byker Sands, man.

Bernard What are you talking about, it says "good condition *plus* good-will".

Dougie What goodwill's that? A lay-by on the A1. Forget it man. Flogging tea in a nylon overall's no life . . .

Bernard I want to explore every avenue . . .

Dougie You'll do that all right. You'll explore every avenue but you won't flog tea and hot dogs in them.

Bernard Look here's another . . . "Cigarette-vending-machine round . . . takings eight hundred pounds a week. Sell, two thousand pounds plus all equipment."

Dougie All equipment. You know what that is. A bunch of keys. When you get there you'll find some bugger's stamped a Government Health Warning on them. No, no, people don't sell *going* concerns, man, that's all a con, if you want to be self-employed why not come in with me?

Bernard 'Cos I'm already *on* Social Security you silly sod.

Dougie But I've got my bit fiddle. House-painting. There's plenty houses want painting up Gosforth. There's buggers up there pay for two coats of gloss and a rub down.

Bernard I'm not a painter.

Dougie Neither am I, but they don't know that, not till the frost comes.

Aunt Ada enters with tea

Ada Here's your tea, me bonny lads.

Dougie By, that's black, did it stir *you?*

Ada I've never been a tea-bag person. Get it down you and be grateful for small mercies.

Bernard Thanks Aunt Ada . . .

Dougie I've seen runnier toffee . . . no wonder you're popular in Ceylon . . .

Ada You've marked the paper like a betting card, son. What are you after?

Dougie He's thinking of going into private enterprise, Ada.

Bernard I'm thinking of starting up on my own.

Ada What as?

Bernard I dunno, but whatever, I'm not sitting back without a fight. (*He states at Dougie*) The collapse of industry has created a vacuum which must now be filled.

Ada Ay, that's right, vacuums must be filled.

Wendy enters

Ad lib greetings: "Hello Pet" . . . etc.

Wendy I could murder a cup of tea.

Dougie Why don't you try this one? It's put up a bloody good fight.

Bernard Have you had a good day, pet?

Wendy Wearing.

Ada Ay, it must be. All that demonstrating and then waitressing, you're on your feet more than's good for you.

Wendy How's it gone here?

Bernard All right

Ada Oh fine, the bairn has to be picked up from across the road, he's been playing with that nice little lad, you know, snotty-nosed thing but canny ... Hi, and our Bernard's surprised us all.

Wendy Oh, what have you done?

Ada Well, he's looking into small businesses.

Bernard Ay, a small business.

Wendy Are you? Have we any capital?

Dougie Just London.

Bernard Look, if we rake together everything we can get our hands on we can invest in a small business. A *working* business. Why should I wait for industry to pick up and beckon me in again. There's fellows down the Club been out of work that long they've lost the inclination to work.

Dougie There's some of them lost the shape as well ...

Bernard I'm determined me now. I've got my back up ... I'm going to *find* a way to make my own living ... and we must rake together every penny ... we can lay hands on ...

Wendy I can make a start, I've got extra work, starting Sunday.

Ada There we are, one door closes, another opens ...

Wendy It'll be regular, it'll mean you making the Sunday dinner ...

Bernard Why, we've all gotta make sacrifices ...

Wendy I'll go and get the bairn.

Wendy goes

Dougie And I'm away to the Club, you coming?

Bernard I'll be down in a minute ...

Dougie (*to Ada*) The Mobile Fanny Craddock ...

Dougie goes

Bernard I'm a bag of nerves, Aunt Ada, but I'm determined to work.

Ada Of course you are, son. You come from a working family. The Robson men never polished the walls with their shoulders. I mind your Uncle John during the depression ...

Bernard I've got to *do* something Aunt Ada ... I've got to *do* something ... not stand about waiting for nowt.

Ada These little businesses sound something like it to me ... seek and you'll find ...

Bernard They all take capital though.

Ada If it's money you need don't be frightened to ask me. I've got a bit put by.

Bernard You've got a right to spend it on yourself.

Ada It would only go to buy a coffin, son ... I've got enough for my needs.

Bernard But you could start living, travel, see the world ...

Ada I've been to Butlins and the Costa del Brava and none of them were all they were cracked up to be ... Now we've got the Metro, I've got the world on my doorstep. So you go out, son, go further afield. Try

other clubs ... and you'll see, something will turn up. Something *always*
turns up—for the Robsons.

Black-out

SCENE 7

Wendy and Buffy are in the dressing-room

Buffy How do you like your dressing-room, kid?
Wendy The facilities aren't very brilliant, are they?
Buffy Wait till you do South Shields Unionist, the dressing-room is
   directly above the urinal ... the fumes work wonders on the make-up
   ... nervous?
Wendy Just a wreck. (*She takes a drink*)
Buffy Don't worry, that's why Buffy's here. Look kid, it's an eight-minute
   cassette, OK? They'd watch you go down on your knees and say a
   prayer for that time.
Wendy What's that growl?
Buffy It's the simultaneous murmurings of five hundred ale-supping
   wankers.
Wendy Oh God!
Buffy Don't worry, it's a good spot this ... wait till you go to Middles-
   borough ... they get to grabbing you and never put you down.
Wendy They won't handle us here, will they Buffy?
Buffy No lovely, no. *You'll* handle them ... you go down to them and give
   them as much as you want to give them ...
Wendy Isn't that dangerous?
Buffy No, now listen to me, if they're reaching out to you, that's danger-
   ous, if you're reaching out to them, that's art. C'mon, siddown, I like to
   leave the stage, get among 'em ... dictate terms ... some clubs don't
   allow it ... depends on the Committee ruling ... This one you're OK,
   so get down there and give it to them ... this is your debut, baby ...
   take control.
Wendy I don't think I can go on ... would you go on for me Buffy?
Buffy Sure I can, I've brought my gear ... but I'd hate myself for it. And
   Harry would never give you another chance ... he's out there intro-
   ducing a new stripper, there'd be hell to pay if an old-timer like me goes
   on. Buck up ... he'll get them in a great mood for you ... he's got a
   knack with the stag audience ...

Black-out

SCENE 8

The stage of the Excelsior Club

Harry comes on stage, with a microphone

Harry Good-evening gentlemen, it's STRIPPERTIME, but before the stripper you've got to have me, a bit of banter before the Fantah. I am delighted to be back in this district with my girls ... somebody said "Will they be safe down there?" I said "They better be, they're the only bodyguard I've got." When they're not stripping I hire them out to Securicorps ... A rough district this, isn't it? I was inoculated before I came here, against *fear!* Nice club this, though, one of the best ... well designed, got the plans from the Berlin Wall ... The beer comes in tankers, the bands come in groups, and the barmaids come in gumshields ... It's a very well-run club though ... What a job I had getting past the doorman ... you've seen him ... looks like a concrete cast of Rocky Marciano ... crumbling. He said to me: "Are you a member?" I said: "No, I'm not a member, I'm a comedian." He said: "We don't need a comedian, we've got fourteen on tonight, there's a Committee Meeting." My God, it's a depressed area this isn't it? The shipyards are dead, dead ... There was a headline in the paper, "Movement on the Tyne"—the tide came in last night. Anybody working here? One? I'll have a sweet and sour takeaway.

Did you hear about the three shipyard workers who went down to the Job Centre. First one ... the feller said "What's your trade?" "Welder." "I can offer you a job on the dustcarts." "God," said the welder, "have I come to this?" Second one went in. "What's your trade?" "Pattern-maker." "I can offer you a job selling doughnuts." "God, have I come to this?" Third one went in. "What's your trade?" "I was a shop steward." "I can offer you a job as lavatory attendant." "Oh great", he said "promotion."

Mind you, people think my job is easy. Being an agent to these strippers. I've got to audition these girls you know ... One woman came along for a job ... she must have been ready for a pension. I said: "Aren't you a bit old for this job?" She said: "I might have winter in my hair, but I've got summer in my heart." "Well, show us what you can do." She started stripping ... first her teeth, then her eyelashes ... I said: "Stop. You might have winter in your hair and summer in your heart but if you don't get a bit of spring up your arse we'll be here till autumn." I had another girl came along ... young lass, very erect ... she stripped off and then played the National Anthem and stood to attention. I said: 'What's that for?" "I've just come out of the Women's Army." "Very good, very good". She put it in her act. Stripped off, played the National Anthem, stood to attention. One night some bugger whistled the Last Post and she fell down dead.

My wife went to see one of them male strippers, she didn't half show off about it ... but she always did hit below the belt. I said: "What did it do for you?" She said: "Eeh, it opened my eyes." I said: "It's a pity it didn't stop your mouth as well." "What did he do with it that was special?" I asked. She said: "He twirled it." "I can twirl mine," I said. "What else did he do?" "He dipped it in my lager." "I can dip mine in your lager, what else did he do?" "He threw it over his shoulder and backheeled it." "That's not fair," I said, "I'm not a bloody footballer." These women know nothing about men, nothing. I said to her, "Name me the three most important parts of a man's body." "Eeh," she said, "the three most important. There's the head." "Yes," I said, "there's the head." "Then there's the heart." "Yes, there's the heart, what's the other one?" "Eeh, I should know, I had it on the tip of my tongue last night." And now gentlemen, it's time for your STRIPPER, so take your hands off your wife's best friend and give a welcome to ... THE WONDER-FUL WANDA ...

Wendy's Act

Halfway through Bernard and Dougie enter the auditorium. Bernard recognizes Wendy

Bernard Wendy!

He rushes on and pushes her off

What are you looking at? ... Bastards ... Think it's funny eh?

Dougie rushes on and they fight

Paulie runs on and chases them off

Harry (*off*) What the hell's going on? Don't just stand there, get the bloody mike on so I can get us out of the shite ...
Paulie (*off*) It's already on.
Harry (*off*) Shit.

Harry comes on stage with a microphone

Gentlemen ... what a finish ... The Wonderful Wanda and Partners ... We'll have another stripper on for you in about fifteen minutes ... unless her taxi breaks down then she'll be here in ten ... Fifteen minutes lads, so top up your glasses, look at that bugger rushing ... what a gut, he looks like a duck ... fifteen minutes lads for more entertainment and another stripper ...

CURTAIN

ACT II

SCENE 1

Bernard's house

Bernard and Wendy are on stage

Bernard Never in my life have I seen anything like it. If I hadn't seen it with my own eyes, I wouldn't *credit* it.

Wendy Are you talking to yourself or do I have to watch the back of your head when we have a conversation?

Bernard I'm talking to *you.*

Wendy Call that talking? You've done nowt but mumble for days.

Bernard And I'll continue, till I get some bloody sense out of it.

Wendy Oh man, I'm getting *sick* of the same refrain.

Bernard My wife stripping eh ... and in front of them animals.

Wendy You watched strippers yourself.

Bernard That's different. They're strippers. You're me wife, *mine.*

Wendy You've always got a tale to suit yourself.

Bernard I cannot get over it. (*He holds out a shaking hand*) Look at the state of that. Me snooker's gone to hell. I cannot put the black on its spot. I'm being talked about and I'm buggered if I can understand it.

Wendy You don't listen very hard when I try to explain.

Bernard Go on then, explain.

Wendy I've tried and tried.

Bernard There's no explanation to making an exhibition of yourself in public, man. I'm amazed I didn't murder you. What if the news had got back? What if the news had infiltrated into Walker? I die to think of it. I just thank God it was Dougie that was with us and not some other bugger ... I've made him bloody swear, on oath ... I would have got the Bible out but it wouldn't have done any good with that sod ... Behind my back. Clandestine arrangements ... I used to think the *News of the World* made these things up ... but it happened. And you would have gone on, eh, if I hadn't stopped you in your tracks ... You'd be doing it yet.

Wendy Yes. I'd be doing it yet. And shall I tell you why, for the last time?

Bernard I've had no explanation up to now that makes any bloody sense ...

Wendy Well, it's because I'm sick to death of toil. Since we've had the bairn I've never stopped. And now you're unemployed I'm not expected to be off my feet. Demonstrating, waitressing, barmaiding. Catching buses here, buses there. Leaving the bairn with Aunt Ada or babysitters or you. Having no family life, no womanhood, no social life, no nowt ...

Bernard You see there's no explanation is there ... no bloody rhyme or reason to it.

Wendy Right Bernard. I'll give you rhyme and reason ... Being a stripper

I can earn more for an eight-minute spot than for a day's work ... being a stripper I can have mornings and afternoons with the bairn and Bernard, being a stripper, I can spend more time building a home.

Bernard And being a better wife I suppose?

Wendy Yes, Bernard, that as well.

Bernard Look you'd end up on your back. You've no idea where it might lead! It's like chocolate fingers, you think "Ooh I'll have one" and you end up eating the whole bloody packet.

Wendy All right, forget it man, Aunt Ada's coming ...

Bernard I'm surprised you can look Aunt Ada in the face.

Wendy Ye gods, Bernard, what have I done? I'm not ashamed of it you know. Nervous I might have been, but ashamed, never.

Bernard Well I'll have to be ashamed for you then, won't I?

Wendy Ashamed for me? But every Sunday morning sees *you* watching strippers!

Bernard I go down the Club with the lads for a couple of pints! The strippers just happen to be on!

Wendy Howay man you watch the strippers—you don't play dominoes. Why? Is it a turn-on for you?

Bernard What the hell are you talking about now?

Wendy You never ask *me* to perform like that.

Bernard Funny bloody marriage I'd have if I asked you to strip in the front room!

Wendy Why? What's the difference in them performing for you? Have I let you down in some way?

Bernard Ay, you've let me down fancying yourself at *that*. You must have done it for yourself.

Wendy I did it for us.

Bernard It wasn't for me. It was behind my back.

A door slams, off

I just thank God it didn't reach Aunt Ada's ears ...

Aunt Ada enters, knocks

Ada Can I come in?

Bernard When did you have to ask if you could come in?

Ada I didn't know if I was interrupting anything.

Bernard Interrupting what?

Ada Well I don't know, do I, but till I do I'll keep knocking.

Bernard Next time I'll get the butler to announce you shall I?

Ada Been to the market. I got you a nice pair of Craister kippers ... real smoked, not them dyed things ...

Wendy Thanks Aunt Ada.

Ada I think it's about time we all had a decent kipper don't you? That what's wrong with the world ... And I've baked you some scones. Get them down you with a bit of jam ... till you liven up a bit.

Bernard She's bloody lively enough from what I've seen!

Ada She's not, she's very quiet, and you're very quiet.

Bernard We can't be singing and dancing all day you know ...
Ada Howway son, what's up? I know there's something up ...
Bernard There's nothing up.
Ada There is, there has been for days. I can see it in your features ... the
Robson men could never disguise their features ... it wasn't in their
nature. Howway, I'm not going to be kept in the dark at my time of life.
Wendy You'd better tell her Bernard ... because if you don't I will ...
Ada Serious is it?
Bernard Bloody.
Ada Who's dead?
Wendy It's not that, Aunt Ada.
Ada Come on then. I didn't wipe your nose all your life for nowt.
Bernard It's her ... she entertains plans to be a *stripper*.
Ada Oooh, does that mean promotion?
Bernard You don't know what I'm saying ... a stripper. Somebody who
takes their bloody clothes off in public.
Ada If she's gonna take that on she'll need to be presentable. You can use
my twin tub for your things.
Bernard There's no danger of *that* ... she has no intention of taking it up.
Not now ... not never!
Ada I don't see why not, she has a nice body you know. I always felt it
was wasted in the café.
Bernard I'm talking about in the clubs. Up on the stage. A professional
stripper.
Ada They'd let you wear flesh-coloured tights?
Wendy No. They don't.
Ada Well, if you've got summat you might as well show it if you can get
paid for it. You would get paid?
Wendy Uhuh ...
Ada There we are, nobody wants anything when it's past its best, I know
... if you're proud of your figure you need never be ashamed of showing
it.
Bernard Well it's not a job I'm proud of her wanting to do.
Ada You men are all alike ... you're proud of using your hands and your
muscles for work but you're ashamed when a woman wants to use her
body. What's proud of being a miner and coughing your lungs out after
forty years down the pit? What's proud of being a soldier and walking
into a hail of machine-gun bullets? What's proud about being a factory
worker then a beggar when you're made redundant?
Bernard I'm going out.

He goes

Ada I shouldn't have said that. Not about being a beggar. But I've seen
too much of the dignity of labour to take any more of it. My uncle Ted
was a red man. A red leader in the shipyard. He used to paint the ships
with red oxide ... inside and out. That paint was everywhere. He was
covered in red. His clothes, his flesh, his pores. 'Course in those days we
didn't know what it was doing to him, but now we know what killed

him. His corpse was like an old paint pot, it could neither rot nor rust. His brother Peter escaped from the shipyards to the Great War. He lasted about five minutes in the trenches.

Wendy But Aunt Ada, he's making me feel in the wrong.

Ada Wrong? For stripping? They've done nowt else but strip the north-east bare. Stripped it of coal, stripped it of ships, stripped it of men and money, so they might as well have the clothes off your back. You need the money. Ay. You go and be a stripper.

Wendy No Aunt Ada. Bernard won't hear of it. He's going out to get the money. He's roused. He's going to get a small business of some sort.

Ada Oh well, if you've stirred him you've done something. They take a bit of rousing, the Robsons, but when they are—watch out!

Black-out

SCENE 2

Outside a C.I.U. Club. Evening

Bernard comes on through the auditorium in a rather cissy nylon overall and hat with a seafood tray. Dougie follows. They ad lib until they reach the Club entrance

Bernard Howway let's try somewhere else. Let's try Scrogg Road man, they get nowt to eat up there!

Dougie Well, is this what you call filling the vacuum left by the collapse of British industry?

Bernard It's better than sitting at home doing nothing.

Dougie That's a matter of opinion. For all the seafood you've sold tonight you might as well be down at the coast feeding the seagulls.

Bernard I don't understand it ... when we used to go drinking we used to *welcome* the seafood man.

Dougie I think it's the good will you bought. The last bloke must have poisoned them.

Bernard Howway then, let's get in.

Dougie No Bernard, you're on your own this time. I've got mates in this club. I divvent want to be seen.

Bernard Selling seafood?

Dougie It's not that. *You're* ashamed to be seen selling seafood. I owe money in there.

Bernard You lying bugger. Nobody ever lent you any money in your life. You're ashamed. Ashamed to be with your mate selling seafood. Here I am, trying to form a respectable business, forging links with the fishing industry ...

Dougie Aa divvent think much of them have come out of the sea ...

Bernard What do you mean? This is best quality seafood off the bed of the sea.

Dougie Bed of the sea. Nuclear bloody dumping ground, Bernard man. It was glowing in the back of the van.

Bernard Bollocks. I've tried it all meself, every one of them, Mussels, whelks, cockles.

Dougie Ay, well divvent go for an X-ray, you might explode.

Bernard Bugger you for your daftness. I'm going in.

Dougie Keep away from the Space Invaders . . .

Bernard goes into the club

Dougie's face tells all

Buffy enters from the club, stands waiting, expostulates

Buffy Shit!

Dougie H'ya darling, can I do anything for you?

Buffy Sure, what you got in mind?

Dougie Oh. Aa divven knaa.

Buffy Now look, smart ass, don't make remarks you can't follow up. OK? You're like a broom without a handle. Got anything else you want to pitch in?

Dougie Oh you're American.

Buffy No, I come from Gateshead, can't you tell? Canadian, all right?

Dougie Oh ay, well that's just ower the watter.

Buffy You know Canada do you?

Dougie No, but my father kept Canadian geese.

Buffy And when did he turn you loose? Look, I know it's testing your powers of observation to the full but have you noticed a girl with a car in the last few minutes? Naah, sorry I asked, go back to sleep. Jesus, look at the time.

Dougie You supposed to be anywhere?

Buffy No, just timing myself, to see how long I can keep up a conversation with you . . . I better call a cab.

Dougie Where do you want to go?

Buffy The Talk of the Tyne.

Dougie I'll get you there.

Buffy Got a magic wand?

Dougie I'll take you.

Bernard enters from the club

Bernard, we're taking this lady to the Talk of the Tyne. You don't mind the smell of fish food do you?

Buffy In my line of business pet, it'll be a welcome relief.

They go

Bernard Dougie man, I'm on a business round! She doesn't want to get in the back with the crabs!

He follows them off

Black-out

SCENE 3

Buffy's flat

Buffy and Dougie enter

Buffy Here we are. Back to the warmth and welcome. It's not much but it's got the finest panorama of the Byker Wall ... Rest awhile, Sir Galahad.

Dougie Hey, mind, I never knew you were a stripper.

Buffy Well, when the Salvation Army turned me down I thought "What the hell". Fix yourself a drink will you? I want to get these clothes off ...

Buffy goes off to the bedroom

Dougie Need any music?

Buffy (*off*) You're in Gateshead now, sonny Jim. Less o' the Walker Wit.

Michelle (*off*) Buffy, Buffy.

Michelle enters

Oh ... company.

Dougie Hello I'm Dougie. Buffy's in there.

Michelle Is she cross?

Dougie What about?

Michelle The transport.

Dougie I brought her home, I think she's all right.

Michelle That's a relief.

Buffy enters

Buffy Where the hell were you? What happened this time?

Michelle The car broke down, Buffy. I had to get help myself.

Buffy I hope it was mental.

Michelle No, carburettor ...

Buffy I was seven minutes late at the Talk of the Tyne ... and didn't the comedian slag me? "Sorry the stripper's late lads, she turned down a one way street out of habit. She couldn't resist the challenge of a NO ENTRY. The stripper'll be here in a minute lads. She stopped by a red light and thought she was home."

Dougie laughs

Michelle I'm dead sorry Buffy, honest I am.

Buffy Now look, get the hell out of here, OK and take this guy with you ... where do you want to go?

Dougie I don't.

Buffy Well you are, where is it?

Dougie Low Walker.

Michelle I'm going over to Westgate, Buffy.

Buffy You're going via Low Walker, now take this guy with you.

Michelle I've gorran appointment, Buffy.

Buffy He can sit and hold it ... I had an engagement at the Talk of the Tyne, so tit for tat, now get out of here.

Michelle All right, come along then, what did you say your name was?

Dougie Dougie, but hi, hang on, I'd rather stay, you asked me for a drink y'know.

Michelle He'd rather stay Buffy ... he'd rather stay ...

Buffy OK suit yourself, but you, beat it, get out of here.

Michelle Will you meet as per usual at Carricks in the morning, Buffy?

Buffy I might see you there if I'm desperate ... Now out ...

Michelle Say you'll come.

Buffy Out.

Michelle Eleven o'clock then ...

Buffy Out.

Michelle scrambles out

Dougie I never expected to see you in a bad temper.

Buffy I'm not ... I'm just angry ... Christ, we strippers don't need much, but we *do need* reliable transport. And even *that ninny* knows that much. Y'know three spots a night, twenty to thirty minutes between each spot, you gotta keep rolling. And taxis cost money.

Dougie You mean your agent doesn't pay?

Buffy Like hell honey. He takes twenty per cent plus VAT, and we still pay the taxi out of what's left. Do you know what my dream is? If there's one left in this crummy life? That some reliable, clean, boring taxi driver will fall madly in love with me ... but they never do ... they might offer terms but I'd rather pay the meter than do a lay on the back seat. Say, how are *you* going to get home?

Dougie I just live ower the watter.

Buffy Ower the watter. You going to swim it? Jump it or just fly it?

Dougie I'll walk. I'm not tired y'see.

Buffy No? What are those red things under your eyes then? War paint?

Dougie They always go like that after midnight.

Buffy All right Cinderella, go at your own pace. I don't mind. I always need to relax after a show. It doesn't do any harm, you sitting with me ...

Pause

Dougie So these taxi drivers make offers eh?

Buffy Sure. All the time. Especially the married ones ...

Dougie Do you ever, er, *succumb*?

Buffy Succumb? That's a nice word for a canny lad. Succumb ... I didn't realize succumb had reached Low Walker.

Dougie You know what I mean.

Buffy Sure. No, I don't succumb. I don't like well-worn upholstery you never know who's been there before you ...

Dougie Do any of the girls do a bit on the side?

Buffy You have found your native tongue, haven't you?

Dougie I just wondered.
Buffy Keep wondering canny lad ... and what about you?
Dougie Me? I've been on the dole since they laid them off at the yard ...
but I do all right.
Buffy All right. What does that mean?
Dougie Well I do a bit you know.
Buffy On the side?
Dougie Painting. House-painting.
Buffy You a painter?
Dougie Not really, but they don't know that till ...
Buffy Till what?
Dougie Just an old joke.
Buffy Try me.
Dougie Till the frost comes ...
Buffy A good line ... I guess it's the way you tell it. How about taking
your hand away. You've got paint under your fingernails.
Dougie Oh ... sorry ...
Buffy I don't know what you've heard about us girls, but we're not into
that ...
Dougie Oh no, I never thought you were ... what the hell are you in it for
then?
Buffy Most of the girls are in it for sound practical boring reasons; you
know, out-of-work husbands, mortgages to pay, plans of opening a little
hat shop in Harrogate ... me, I just drifted into it.
Dougie How?
Buffy Does it matter?
Dougie To me it does.
Buffy My, you have got heroic overtones tonight, haven't you?
Dougie I'd just like to know.
Buffy OK you will know. Whether you believe it or not are two different
things. I came over here to hitchhike round the place, look up my
Scottish ancestry, dig up the roots ... floated down to the Edinburgh
Festival, made a fool of myself in Street Theatre, drifted down here,
drifted into stripping and I'll drift on eventually I expect.
Dougie Not just yet though eh?
Buffy Not just yet ... Shouldn't you be trekking back to ... Low Walker
now?
Dougie I thought you might have asked us to stay.
Buffy What for?
Dougie Ye knaa ...
Buffy You could sand down the windows but you might keep the neigh-
bours awake.
Dougie Ye knaa what I mean.
Buffy No, I will never know what a Geordie means till he learns how to
ask.
Dougie I'm asking then. I'm looking appealing.
Buffy You're looking downright doggish. Get out of here.
Dougie You can't mean that—it's half-past one in the morning.

Buffy I mean it round the clock. Here, payment for your trouble. (*She offers him some money*)
Dougie Oh I divvent want that.
Buffy You've got to take it, it's a strict sense of propriety amongst us girls.
Dougie I don't care, I'm not taking it.
Buffy You've done the taxi-driver out of a job, you blackleg ...
Dougie I'd better take it then. (*He takes the money*) When can I see you again?
Buffy Tuesday I'm at Rockshotts, Wednesday at the Westgate Video Club, Friday at the Benwell British Legion ...
Dougie No, you know what I mean.
Buffy I don't again.
Dougie Well can I pick you up some time? And take you out?
Buffy In that fish van?
Dougie Oh no, that's not mine. I've got a proper van for my paint round ...
Buffy I'm not going out with any turpentine pirate ... Good-night ...
Dougie I'll see you again though ...
Buffy Good-night.
Dougie Tuesday at Rockshotts was it?
Buffy Good-night.

He goes

Black-out

SCENE 4

Wendy's and Bernard's bedroom. Night

Wendy (*in bed*) Bernard, is that you?

Bernard enters

Bernard Of course it's me.
Wendy I thought it was burglars.
Bernard Burglars, they'd get nowt here.
Wendy You never know.
Bernard If a burglar broke in here he'd leave us a tip.
Wendy Are you coming to bed?
Bernard I'm just going to get this stink of fish off.
Wendy Come on, don't be silly. You're late tonight. Have you stayed in one of the clubs?
Bernard Stayed in one of the clubs? I'm working them, man, not staying in them.
Wendy I thought you might stay at the bar?
Bernard What? And drink the sodding profits?
Wendy No need to use that language in the bedroom.
Bernard You what?
Wendy There's no need to swear in the bedroom.

Bernard There's every sodding need to swear in the bastard bedroom.

Wendy If the job's going to worry you, give it up.

Bernard Isn't that just like a woman all over. Give it up. Don't you know it's an investment? It's a business. I've got money tied up in it. Well I've got Aunt Ada's money tied up in it. "You can close the shipyard gates, stop the pithead wheel turning, but you can't stop a Robson". But the bastards stopped me. They've got Aunt Ada's money and all.

Wendy She'd rather it went trying to do something.

Bernard That's bloody helpful isn't it? I mean, it's only a lifetime's savings. I even had to pay for the plastic trays. Some business man I am.

Wendy Don't undermine yourself.

Bernard Oh, I'm undermined, me. Fish-seller ... When we were lads, we used to laugh at the fish-seller from North Shields. But at least his were fresh. Mine might be made of rubber for all they sell.

Wendy Bernard, Bernard ...

Bernard I cannot make it pay. It's no good. And the clubs, I hate the bloody clubs. I used to be a member but now I'm nowt. Some I'm even not allowed to go in, others I'm expected to give the doorman a back-hander. And when I do get me way in, I'm lucky if I sell owt. You'll be happy now.

Wendy I'm not happy, Bernard.

Bernard You've been watching us since I started to see if I'd make a mess at it. You've been frigid towards us since I tried to make a go of it.

Wendy Not true, love. I know you're having a bad time of it. If it hurts, man, show me. Tell me if it's too much for you.

Bernard I can't make it pay. I cannot make it work, that fish round. Now say it. Go on, say it.

Wendy I'm saying nothing, except that you've done your best. And what you've done, you've done for your family.

Bernard You don't know what a mess we're in.

Wendy Well, we're in it together, love. You can show me the books later, but don't be afraid to show me how you feel now. You were always like this, you know. The first time we met in that swimming pool at Whitley Bay, you had to go diving off the top board. I could see you were terrified but you insisted on doing it. Sheer bravado. You hit the water like a sack of coal, but came up thinking you were Tarzan. I didn't mind. I liked it, but there's no need for it now. We have the bairn to think of. We'll get by.

Bernard Did I bring you to this? Scratching and scraping?

Wendy You did well. We've got a house and furniture.

Bernard Not that it's paid for.

Wendy We'll pay for it.

Bernard And we've got to pay Aunt Ada back.

Wendy We'll pay her back.

Bernard What on, fresh air? God, to think I brought you to this. Do you know, when I was on that diving-board, I thought you were a film-star.

Wendy Well, I wasn't. I was a shop assistant and a weekend beauty queen.

Bernard With your looks, you might have got decent offers.

Wendy I got offers all right, but not many of them decent. In fact, Bernard, of all the offers I got then, yours was the best. Now pull yourself together. We won't starve. You did your best, now it's my turn. You know, you do smell of fish.

Bernard Should I go and have another shower?

Wendy I'll put up with it if it's the last time. Are you coming in?

Bernard Ay...

Wendy Should I put this book away?

Black-out

SCENE 5

The Club—Concert Room

Michelle's Jungle Act

The act ends with three shots fired from the wings—she flounders about and finally expires on the chair

Black-out

The Lights come up on the Club Lounge

Buffy and Cilla are sitting at the bar; the barmaid is behind the bar

Harry enters and comes to them

Harry Did you see that? Did you see that? (*To the Barmaid*) Large one, pet. I have a sudden feeling my books are overstocked.

Cilla Have you, Harry?

Harry She drags me out to see her new act, drags me away from the comforts of home, to present me with that bloody rubbish.

Cilla Not pleased were we not, Harry?

Harry Not pleased? There was so much gunfire going off the audience thought World War Three had started!

Buffy It was enterprising, Harry ... perhaps she wants a little drama in her act.

Harry Drama ... she's here to give them a hard on, not a bloody heart attack!

Cilla Give her a break—she's inventive, Harry.

Harry Inventive. I wouldn't put it past her to have someone swing on in a Tarzan skin with her hanging on to his cobblers to make the screams sound realistic.

Wendy enters

Wendy Hello everyone ... (*To Buffy*) Have you had a word with Harry?

Buffy Yes, but you could have chosen a better moment.

Wendy I'll go.

Buffy Brave it out honey.

Wendy Hello, Harry ... Buffy said you might be free to have a word.

Harry I suppose you want me to give you another chance?

Wendy Yes please, Harry.

Harry You've worked it all out with your husband have you?

Wendy Yes.

Harry He's quite agreeable? He's not going to throw any more hysterics when your bra comes off?

Wendy No.

Harry Your mother-in-law isn't going to object? Your granny? The kids' school-teacher?

Wendy It's all fine.

Harry No snags, no drawbacks? Because this is your last chance . . .

Wendy Fine.

Harry No stipulations whatsoever?

Wendy I'd rather not strip in Low Walker.

Harry I knew that was coming. Right you're on Sunday, Byker and Heaton Social, Byker Iniskilling, Byker Top and Byker Bottom, how does that grab you?

Wendy Great.

Harry And if you're still alive after that lot, maybe they'll give you the freedom of the Byker Wall.

Michelle enters

Michelle Well, I thought despite a few hiccups that went rather well!

Harry What the bleeding hell have you been drinking?

Michelle Lager and blackcurrant.

Harry Bloody hell, are you not tempting providence?

Michelle I never tempt anybody Harry.

Harry You can bloody say that again.

Michelle (*to the girls*) Well, you two've not said much. What did you think? Buffy?

Harry Why don't you ask me. I'm the arbitrator of good taste round here. And I thought it was crap. What the hell was all that bloody twitching? I thought you had St Vitus' Dance.

Michelle No, I was dying, Harry.

Harry In more ways than one.

Michelle I can see you're confused, Harry. You see the record's called "Maneater"—tigers you see, Harry—did you know that seventy-five per cent of the world's population of tigers are now extinct, so I thought it'd be really good to do a strip about dead tigers 'cos it's relevant to world wildlife preservation.

Harry There weren't many people out there thought you were a man-eater. And you didn't look worth preserving.

Buffy Ease off, Harry.

Harry Ease off? I haven't even bloody started yet. If you're going to use jungle music why don't you do the job properly for Christ's sake. Get a snake and be done with it, with a bit of luck the bloody thing might strangle you. Right, who am I taking to Easington Colliery Miners' Welfare?

Cilla Me Harry.
Harry Thank God it's not *her*, they'd all go out on strike again.

Harry stalks off with Cilla

Michelle Do you think he meant it?
Buffy About the act?
Michelle About the snake.
Buffy I think he meant something.
Michelle I don't mind you know. I've always fancied a snake.
Harry (*off*) Come on you ...

She goes

Wendy Want a drink?
Buffy Yes. Vodka and tonic.
Wendy (*to the barmaid*) Vodka and tonic please.
Buffy Well kid, you're on.
Wendy Yes.
Buffy This time it's for real. You better stick very close to Buffy this week.
Wendy Don't you worry, Buffy, I will.
Buffy Do you have time to work on your routine?
Wendy Yes, Bernard is staying at home till I get it sorted out. And he's got a nice aunt to take care of him.
Buffy That's what we all need, the nice aunt.
Wendy I've got you.
Buffy Then you better stick close kid, you're gonna need me.
Wendy You bet I will.

Dougie enters in a ravishing white suit

Buffy Hi, look what the wind's blown in, you look smart, going into the ice-cream business?
Dougie I wanted to have a word with you, if that's all right?
Buffy Take a pew, we'll cancel our conversation.
Wendy I'll go and leave you to it.
Buffy Be realistic, there's nothing to be left to ...
Wendy All the same, I've never seen Dougie look like that ... See you ... Tara Dougie.

She goes

Dougie I've got a proposition to put to you!
Buffy Marriage, I'll put you on the list.
Dougie No, I've been to see Harry.
Buffy You're going to be a male stripper, hey, good for you ... have you got what it takes?
Dougie Driver, your driver.
Buffy In the back of your van? No thanks, I'm stiff with varnish as it is.
Dougie I've sold the van and bought a car.
Buffy Did you get that suit out of the difference?
Dougie Howway, I'm being serious.

Buffy My driver, my personal driver. No kidding?
Dougie No kidding.
Buffy You're on, ten pounds a session.
Dougie The money's not important.
Buffy Ten pounds a round trip, standard rate, I'm not letting the neighbours talk.
Dougie I'd do it for nothing, I would.
Buffy I know a lot of girls like you. When do I get to see this car then?
Dougie Now, I'll bring it round the front. Two minutes.
Buffy Sure you wouldn't like to be a male stripper? You could do a spot between my acts . . .
Dougie Come off it . . .
Buffy OK . . . stick to the steering wheel . . . but I'd audition you any time up at my place in that suit . . . whoo!

Black-out

SCENE 6

Bernard's house — the kitchen. Evening

Aunt Ada and Bernard are on stage. Bernard is making the dough for bread

Ada That's right. Give it a good stir Bernard.
Bernard My you need a strong arm.
Ada You cannot make a stotty without a good bit of arm work. Now prepare your board. Flour it lightly. I've always said men could make good cooks if they put their mind to it. The Robson men could always turn their hand to cooking. I mind when your Grand-Uncle Bill, in the nineteen twenty-three Depression, made seaweed soup to keep his family from the workhouse. Ay, he did. He walked down to Tynemouth and collected a bagful of seaweed and limpets and winkles and made a pot full of soup for his family. They were all bad for a week but he tried. And after that they'd eat owt, believe me.
Bernard What now Aunt Ada?
Ada Knead it . . . you'll be good at that . . . being strong. Are your hands clean? With your knuckles, that's the way, go on give it a hammering. It's good to have the "Bero" recipe book out again, we Robson girls were all taught out of the "Bero" recipe book. New cake, stotty bread, fadges, drop scones, butterfly cakes . . . bread and butter pudding . . . I tried to teach your mother you know, but she could never adapt being a southern girl . . . her heart was never in Newcastle and when your father died I said "You might as well go back to Darlington where you belong. But for God's sake", I said, "leave our Bernard here to be brought up a Robson."
Bernard I'm glad she did, Aunt Ada.
Ada She said she'd send for you when she settled. But they're wanderers in Darlington, always have been, always will be, and when she married

a railwayman nobody was surprised. Let's see that, give it the pinching test ... ay, that'll do, put it by the fire and let it rise for an hour. I've got a bottle of brown ale in for you ... you've deserved it ...

Bernard goes off

Ada gets a bottle out from her bag

Bernard returns

Bernard That stage over ...
Ada A bit to go yet ... after it's proved ... you'll have to give it a second kneading, then I'll show you how to roll it out and prove it again ...
Bernard It's a long job.
Ada You don't mind do you?
Bernard No, I'm enjoying meself.
Ada Here's your beer. Is it all right?
Bernard Yes.
Ada I don't know what goes in it nowadays. Before the war it tasted more of hops and alcohol ... mind it doesn't blow you up ...

Wendy enters

Wendy Hello ... I didn't know you'd still be here, Aunt Ada.
Ada I've brought me "Bero" recipe book. Bernard wanted to know how to make bread.
Wendy Make bread, at this time of night ...
Bernard Best time man, pastry rises in the heat of the house.
Wendy Well, what next? I wonder.
Ada There's no end to it. But I always said, "The Robson men can do anything if they put their minds to it." I'll have a look and see if it's rising ... then I'll put me coat on and let meself out.

She goes off

Wendy Bread eh?
Bernard If it works it'll prove economical.
Wendy It'll work Bernard. It'll work.
Bernard It should do ... Aunt Ada's dug the family recipe book out ... look at that, would you credit it? First published nineteen twenty-eight.
Wendy Blimey, it's like living with history living with Aunt Ada.
Bernard It is ... this house is going to smell like Hadrian's Bakery ...
Wendy Hadrian's Bakery?
Bernard They were the bakers in Walker when I was a kid ... they're not there now but we always used to get a sticky bun coming out from school ... smashing it was.

Ada enters

Ada It's rising nicely, Bernard. Give it half an hour then do as I said, or follow the book. I'll be going to see if my house is still standing.
Wendy Thanks Aunt Ada ...

Ada goes

Bernard Always there in time of need, Aunt Ada.
Wendy She is.
Bernard How did you get home?
Wendy By Metro.
Bernard Don't they provide transport this time of night?
Wendy They do when I start work, but it comes out of me own money.
Bernard How do you feel about starting?
Wendy All right.
Bernard You know I've still got my doubts about all this?
Wendy You're bound to ...
Bernard Say the word and I'll put a stop to it yet ...
Wendy We've had all that out ... I feel all right about it ...
Bernard If I could change it I would.
Wendy I'm sure you would.
Bernard Ay, well, you still love us then?
Wendy Still love you? That's the first time you've asked that in many a long day.
Bernard We were younger then and I was working.
Wendy Ay, I still love you.
Bernard I'll go and see if the bread's rising.
Wendy Haven't you forgotten something?
Bernard I love you an' all.

He goes off

(*Off*) It is! It is!

Bernard enters

It's doing like Aunty Ada said.
Wendy Yes, it would do ...
Bernard Well, you're home now, I suppose I can go out.
Wendy If you have a mind ...
Bernard I'm not bothered ... I can understand how you women get house-bound ... when I was working I couldn't wait to get home and get out to the Club, now I'm not bothered ...
Wendy Why, are you ashamed of not working?
Bernard Why, half the buggers down there don't work ... but with you bringing the money in ...
Wendy Well, their wives are supporting them.
Bernard Oh ay, in a way, but with you it's different ... I mean ...
Wendy Stripping? You still cannot bring yourself to say it can you?
Bernard Why ay, it's all right.
Wendy Go on then, say it ...
Bernard Ay, striptease ...
Wendy Striptease, you sound very coy, striptease ... it's like Pin-Up Girl, Cheesecake ... I'm stripping Bernard, get that into your head and accept it ... it's a career.

Bernard Ay, you'll be in the Honours List next.
Wendy Don't say what I'll be, and what you'll be, what I'm doing, what
you're up to ... this is a mutual thing Bernard ... a family thing, for
me, you and the bairn ...
Bernard Ay, well that side is your life, you know the rules ...
Wendy It's our life Bernard ... when I shut that door to go to work, I
don't want to be banging it in your face ... when I come back in I don't
want to pretend that what I'm doing doesn't belong ... we're all one
... some of the girls have husbands who watch their act, encourage
them, back them up, train them even ...
Bernard Where, behind drawn curtains?
Wendy I don't mind locking the neighbours out, Bernard ... but we don't
want curtains between us ...
Bernard What am I supposed to do?
Wendy Well for a start, smile about it ... then take an interest ... we're
not swapping roles Bernard, just taking on each other's responsibilities
for a while ...

The baby cries, off

Bairn crying. Try and get him back to sleep, if not put a bottle on ...
Bernard Hey. I'm not titty feeding yet ... you're home, it's your job.

He storms out

Black-out

SCENE 7

Buffy alone in pub or club lounge. Barmaid behind bar

Cilla enters

Cilla Can I join you?
Buffy It's a public place, baby.
Cilla What you doing here on Thursday?
Buffy Just thinking about Friday.
Cilla You're up to something, I *know*.
Buffy Your nose is right again, Cill. I'm dressing Wendy.
Cilla The Wondrous Wanda.
Buffy The same.
Cilla Think she'll make it? I'm only asking.
Buffy Time and Byker will tell.
Cilla She's got all the moves I must admit, but that's about all ...
Buffy The rest might come.
Cilla Don't you think Harry's taking on far too many girls? I'm only
asking.
Buffy There's work for us all, Cilla.
Cilla I wouldn't be too sure about that, he's taking them straight from
school now.

Buffy Just the Convent girls.

Cilla He plucks them off out the dole queue.

Buffy If nobody else wants them he's got the right to make an offer.

Cilla Scandalous I call it, I was nineteen when I started.

Buffy That was in the Golden Era, Cilla ... the pioneering days.

Cilla And I'd had experience of life.

Buffy Don't worry Cill, some of the punters will always prefer maturity to the coy charms of gym-slipped youth.

Cilla Bloody schoolgirls, and they come on as if they'd had it ...

Buffy We're like Hitler's Army, Cilla, being pushed on from behind by the elite Virgin Corps.

Cilla You don't give a sod, that's obvious ... if things go wrong you'll be back in Canada quick as a flash, marrying a millionaire ...

Buffy The Tyne can be crossed even by natives, what's to keep you here?

Cilla I couldn't leave and do my work among strangers, you'd never know who'd be in the audience.

Michelle enters with a bag

Michelle I've got him.

Buffy Got who?

Michelle Rupert ...

Cilla Who's Rupert when he's whitewashed?

Michelle Take a look ... Rupert.

Cilla (*looking in the bag*) For goodness sake, a snake ...

Michelle Keep your voice down, Cilla, people are very peculiar about these things.

Buffy How unusual, is he dead?

Michelle No, he's just asleep, how do you like him?

Cilla Love him I must say.

Buffy How long is he?

Michelle Well I bought him as a five-footer, but I've had the tape to him and I only make it four and a half. A bit disappointing.

Cilla I know the feeling.

Buffy What do you feed this guy on?

Michelle Mice or rabbits.

Buffy Rabbits, dead rabbits?

Michelle No, alive ones ... you just get them by the ears, hold them up and *gulp* they're down ... *etc. ad lib*

Buffy What a bed mate eh?

Michelle Yes. He likes coming to bed. He likes the warmth of my body ...

Cilla Are you going to use him in your act?

Michelle Of course I am, I thought the men might like him.

Buffy They're not supposed to *like* him. He's supposed to *rouse* them ... the snake is the ultimate in *phallic symbolism.*

Michelle The dirty buggers ... hear what they're saying about you, Rupert?

Buffy You better get another bag, here comes his mate ...

Paulie enters

Paulie Hello girls.

Michelle Hello Paulie.
Cilla Hello Paul.
Buffy Hello Paulie, do you fancy a rabbit?
Paulie You what?
Cilla Take no notice Paul.
Paulie I won't don't worry. It's how I get on ... now, Michelle, you've got something new to show me.
Michelle Yes, Paulie, my new act ...
Paulie Good, good. New acts is to be encouraged. (*To the Barmaid*) C'mon pet, Courvoisier brandy and soda. One for yourself.
Michelle Meet Rupert.

Paulie passes away in a faint ...

Cilla Paulie! There, there Paulie ... thank God ... he's coming round ... you daft bugger, he could have hit his head.
Paulie What in God's name was that?
Michelle Rupert.

Paulie faints again

Oh, he doesn't like we, Rupert.
Paulie Take it away, get out of my sight ... go ... go.
Cilla For God's sake take it away.
Buffy Time for walkies, Rupert.

Michelle goes

The girls ad lib "He's only a little harmless python ... " etc.

Cilla Come on Paul, stand up. They're gone ... you must be allergic to them ... we all have a bit of weakness ...
Paulie What a thing ...
Buffy Worry you do they, Paulie?
Paulie I wasn't frightened of them. I just got a bit of a surprise, that's all.
Cilla Come on, you better come with me ... I've got something to show you as well ...
Paulie Does it move?
Buffy Only in the line of business ...
Cilla You're shaking like a leaf. What did it do?
Paulie It licked me with its tongue.

They go

Dougie enters

Dougie Buff. Thank God I've caught you alone.
Buffy What do you mean? We're always alone.
Dougie I know, but this is different, just the two of us ...
Buffy Should we form a quorum?
Dougie I think we should have something out.
Buffy Lower your voice or we'll be expelled.
Dougie I've got something to put to you. Of importance I think.

Buffy You've sold the transport?

Dougie Would I do a thing like that?

Buffy I dunno, would you?

Dougie It's my privilege taking you round your spots, all those drunken buggers, I'm at the back ready to protect you.

Buffy Is *that* what you're doing back there?

Dougie What the hell do you think I'm doing?

Buffy Well I don't know. I've often wondered, because you pay little attention to my act.

Dougie That's because I *like* you, man.

Buffy Oh, do you want me chaste, then?

Dougie I want you as you are ... but Aa divvent want to see too much of you—yet. What you do is for them who've paid ... I avert my eyes to all that.

Buffy When do you bring your eyes to bear then, Dougie?

Dougie I'm all eyes for you now and you know it, so I wondered, is there any chance?

Buffy Chance of what?

Dougie Well, you know.

Buffy I might know but I want to hear it.

Dougie You and me man.

Buffy What, dominoes, pool, bingo...?

Dougie Living together ... getting married even.

Buffy Are you offering me marriage, Dougie?

Dougie If it'll make you happy, yes. Well, what do you think?

Buffy I've got one or two conditions.

Dougie You're bound to, women's like that, aren't they?

Buffy Not up here they ain't.

Dougie Go on then, out with it ... but mind I'm not leaving Walker.

Buffy Not even for Canada?

Dougie Canada's all right, but Gateshead's out the bloody question.

Buffy All right, that's *your* condition ... now mine ... you've got to be able to say, "I love you Buffy".

Dougie But I do!

Buffy But you never *say* it ... you say "I like yer", or "Aa think you're canny" but you don't say, ... "I love you". Go on, say it.

Dougie You're making me sound a right whoofter now ... But all right. I love you.

Buffy Good, I'll expect that said every day. Second, I will not be addressed as "man", neither will I be "The Missis". I shall be Buffy, Beverley, or darling, dearest, "my esteemed wife".

Dougie You're putting obstacles in the way now.

Buffy Finally, as to status, I shall expect to be put before, or in preference to, the *Club*, the *snooker*, the *match*, the *lads*, the *booze* ...

Dougie Do you want to turn me into a monk?

Buffy If you're willing to fulfil those conditions you can go out and buy a ring ... a cheap one, we'll be economizing ...

Dougie Do you not think it might be easier to just live together?

Buffy Not in Walker. That bend in the river is not conducive to a loose relationship.
Dougie Ay, well, that'll have to do ...

Wendy enters with a bag

Wendy Hello you two, Dougie.
Buffy Tell her then ... and be gracious.
Dougie We're getting married ...
Wendy Never!
Dougie It was nearly that an' all.
Wendy Oh congratulations.
Dougie I'm not so sure about that ...
Buffy Get on with you man, before I change my mind ...
Dougie What size is your finger?
Buffy Standard downpipe ... size H.
Dougie Do you not want to come and choose it with me?
Buffy No, I've done too much choosing in my life.
Dougie I'll go then.
Buffy You do that.
Dougie To the Ring Shop.
Buffy Go!
Dougie Right ... engagement.
Buffy *Wedding!*

He goes

Wendy That's wonderful Buff.
Buffy Is it? You tell me. You married a Walker lad ...
Wendy Yes, they're canny lads down there, trouble is they never stop telling one another. I'm surprised at you taking on Dougie though.
Buffy So was he.
Wendy Well you certainly spring surprises.
Buffy Well, I've got another one. Dirty Harry's on his way.
Wendy *Harry?*
Buffy Sure, he wants to see how you're shaping up.
Wendy Oh no!
Buffy Don't look so dismayed, it's his money. He's got to see what he's laying it on.
Wendy Don't talk like that, Buffy, you make it sound like Bernard's worst fears.
Buffy Berny still has fears, has he?
Wendy It haunts him.
Buffy Why doesn't he look at it in broad daylight, then maybe it won't be so spooky.
Wendy I've tried and I've tried, but no, he keeps saying he'll get a job, things'll change.
Buffy You better tell Bernard the only thing that's gonna change around here is you.
Wendy Oh, I'll not change.

Buffy Oh yes you will, honey. They'll do it for you. When you stand up in front of that pack, you produce something inside you you didn't know was there. It happens as a defence, as a protection. When those guys are gazing up your fanny, they're not exactly showering you with respect. That you've got to maintain for yourself. Nice girls go typing, they stay nice girls. Nice girls go stripping, and honey, they change. You enter an area where your husband can't follow. Sure you can still love him, but if you think it's just a matter of him staying at home making the Sunday lunch or putting the kids to bed, forget it, because you're kidding yourself. It's a different ball game, baby, so if you don't like the rules, get back to the kitchen.

Bernard enters

Buffy Well, Bernard, enter the dizzy realms of show business.
Bernard I thought I'd pick you up.
Wendy That's good, but I've got to wait and see Harry.
Bernard You mean in this place?
Buffy We're like street traders, Bernard, it's all done on the side. Talk nicely to her. It's the best present a feller can give a girl up here on Tyneside. I'll hang on for you.

Buffy exits

Bernard She's too smart for her own good.
Wendy She's a professional
Bernard Don't model yourself on her.
Wendy I could do worse.
Bernard Of course, she's the one who trained you. She's been your guide and mentor.
Wendy As a matter of fact, she has.
Bernard And who trained her, I wonder.
Wendy I think she trained herself.
Bernard I'll bet she bloody did. Now that is my idea of a stripper.
Wendy You have your idea of what a stripper is then?
Bernard Ay, and not far wrong, I'm sure.
Wendy But Bernard, I'm meeting them all the time, I'm working with them, they're canny lasses. They run around like housemaids and get as little thanks.
Bernard Their whole life is thanks. "Thanks for doing nowt, now do it again."
Wendy You've just seen them from the audience. It looks easy, but they've put a lot into it, it's their work.
Bernard Work? That's not work. I spent five years as an apprentice learning a trade ... and I'm worth nowt. You take your clothes off in eight minutes and you get two hundred pounds a week.
Wendy That's where the market is.
Bernard Ay, the cattle market.
Wendy Ah, Bernard, not here.
Bernard The Technical College handed me a diploma for my craft, you

know. Centre lathe turner. You'd better have a card to take its place
... gilt-edged, Exotic Dancer, highly skilled, four days' training.

Wendy Don't take your bitterness out on me.

Bernard It's enough to make you bitter. "Learn a trade", it's been the
family motto. "The Robson men were always craftsmen." "If you've got
a skill at your fingertips son you'll always be needed." What a myth.
The empty shipyards are mocking ten thousand craftsmen. I can take
you into any club in the area and point out the most skilled men of their
day—finished—on the scrapheap, like me. And I've got to tell them it's
you who's been given work ... *work!* "Bugger the craftsmen, bugger the
skills, get your clothes off missis, you're in work."

Wendy It's the only work that's going to be offered to this house for many
a long day. Face the facts Bernard. *You're* out of work. You might be
out of work for years, but while I've got a good body I can use it to
make a living. Look, even if you're working in a factory you're selling
your body. Anyway, it's better than being a waitress, a cleaner or a
skivvy till I'm worn out ...

Bernard You always fancied yourself at it, once a beauty queen always a
beauty queen, show them your number, show them your figure, show
them every bloody thing, call that a job?

Wendy It's how you do it makes it a job. If you'd come and see me work
you'd see that. You'd see I'm not doing it for *them* or for *me*, you'd see
I'm doing it for us, the whole family ... I mean to them, I'm this
stripper, The Wonderful Wanda ... but you'd see, to you, I'd be your
Wendy.

Bernard Wonderful Wanda ... little Wendy ... *I'm* not allowed the luxury
of a split personality ... I'm bloody Bernard everywhere I go. You want
to change, that's the top and bottom of it ... being with them others
has lured you on ... you *want* to change, let's face it ...

Wendy All right, of all the changes I've been offered this is the one I find
most attractive.

Bernard There we are, at last ...

Wendy The other is the weekly wait for the handout and one night at the
Bingo ... look around you, people are being worn out for not being
wanted. They're losing faith in themselves. I can feel it happening to us
... if stripping for a living gives this family any purpose for God's sake
let's take it. This is our last chance to step out ... give life a go instead
of being a burden. Come with me, show what we can do together. Be
my escort, my driver, my bodyguard, my partner, my everything, my
man. There's only shame and humiliation when we're apart.

Harry enters

Harry Come on then, have you owt to show us?

Wendy Oh Harry, you know me husband, Bernard?

Harry Oh ay. Have you owt to show us then?

Wendy Yes, Harry, I hope you like it.

Harry I better like it. They don't bugger about in Byker.

Wendy Do you mind if Bernard waits?

Harry It'll only take eight minutes. That's not going to stretch him, is it?
Wendy Oh ... no.
Harry Howway then.

They exit

The tabs close

SCENE 8

Harry is onstage in front of the curtains giving the after-dinner speech at a Rotarians' function

Harry Mr President, Gentlemen, fellow Rotarians, may I say how honoured and delighted I am to be invited to address you. The subject I have chosen to speak on is my personal business, which is, as I'm sure a lot of you are aware, the presentation and representation of Exotic Dancers, known to you lads of course as *Strippers*.

 Like all of us here I'm a business man and I follow the law of supply and demand. And when I say "demand", gentlemen, I'm not joking because as far as strippers are concerned, the north-east is screaming out for them. I think, in fact, I would go as far as to say that stripping is a public need, just as much as health, housing and education. And I think I can safely say that I, in my humble way, help to satisfy that need. I am proud to say that I run the biggest agency in the north-east and I run it properly. I am sure you have heard the word "exploitation" used regarding agents in their dealings with the girls. Well, all I can say is when I hear the word "exploitation" I reach for my books, and on those books I have eighty-three full-time strippers and more clamouring to get on every day. And, gentlemen, those girls are like daughters to me. I think I can safely say that I get more cards on Father's Day than anyone running an orphanage.

 I can safely say to any girl interested in pursuing an artistic career that even in hard times, that in the stripping industry, the level of employment is constant. For when things are hard in the home, that is exactly the time when the ordinary man needs some form of relief. When the money stops, gentlemen, love flies out the window. I'm very proud of the fact, gentlemen, that following Rotarian principles of the concept of service, when other industries are hit by strife or recession, I am usually the first to lend support. For instance, during the Miners' Strike, my organization took a leaf out of the travel agents' brochures and offered cut-price stripping packages—five girls for the price of four, with, I might add, a comic thrown in.

 These, gentlemen, are facts I'm giving you and I work on facts, not prejudice and romantic notions. I think I can safely say that the stripping industry has become a phenomenon over the last twenty years. Frankly, the stripping industry has replaced the shipping industry. In fact, if you were to go into any Working Men's Club at this moment in time you-would be sure to find that one of my girls would be doing her act.

Harry exits, as:

The main tabs open, revealing, behind a gauze curtain, Wendy with her back to the audience. She does her strip facing this way

Wendy's Strip

At the end of the strip, there is applause as Wendy puts on her wrap and looks into the wings

Wendy Bernard?

The voice of the Club Secretary is heard off, over a booming mike

Club Secretary (*off*) That was your first strip of the day, the first ever public performance of The Wonderful Wanda. She shows more promise than Paddy's mare and I think she's going to develop and we'll all be here to see her. Now don't run away because we'll have another stripper back in twenty minutes. The Sensuous Samantha who does her act with handcream, a really slippery one that. Now show a bit of appreciation for these lasses, they do a grand job. Well done, Wonderful Wanda ...

CURTAIN

FURNITURE AND PROPERTY LIST

ACT I

SCENE 1

On stage: For Cilla's Act:
Shimmery curtain
Club Lounge:
Bar. *Behind it:* bottles of drink, glasses, etc. *On bar:* ashtrays, beermats
Bar stools
Tables. *On them:* ashtrays, beermats
Chairs
Stools

Personal: **Wendy:** handbag with money
Ada: handbag with money
Bernard: money in pocket
Dougie: money in pocket
Paulie: rings on fingers (required throughout)

SCENE 2

On stage: Tables. *On them:* ashtrays
Chairs
Counter. *On and behind it:* coffee/tea machine, cups, saucers, plates, cutlery, food including chocolate biscuits
Cloth for **Wendy**

SCENE 3

On stage: Table. *On it:* pot of tea, mug, note
Dining-chairs
2 armchairs
Electric fire
Sideboard. *In it:* tablecloth, crockery, cutlery

Personal: **Wendy:** handbag with business card

SCENE 4

On stage: Desk. *On it:* telephone, papers, pens, etc.
Several chairs

SCENE 5

On stage: 1 chair

Off stage: Bag, tape recorder with tape (**Michelle**)
Bag, new tape recorder, tapes (**Wendy**)
Bag, tape (**Buffy**)
Flags (**Michelle**)

SCENE 6

On stage: As Scene 3 but table clear

Off stage: Newspaper (**Bernard**)
              3 cups of tea (**Ada**)

SCENE 7

On stage: Table. *On it:* mirror, **Wendy's** bag, clothes, make-up, etc., bottle of
              drink
              Chair
              Buffy's bag

SCENE 8

On stage: Shimmery curtain

Off stage: Microphone (practical) (**Harry**)—required twice

ACT II

SCENE 1

On stage: As Act I, Scene 6

Off stage: Bag with pair of kippers, wrapped, bag of scones (**Ada**)

SCENE 2

On stage: C.I.U. Club sign outside entrance to club

Off stage: Seafood tray (**Bernard**)

Personal: **Buffy:** bag, wrist-watch

SCENE 3

On stage: Settee
              Drinks table. *On it:* bottles of drink, glasses

Personal: **Buffy:** bag, wrist-watch, money

SCENE 4

On stage: Double bed and bedding
              Bedside table. *On it:* lamp
              Book for **Wendy**

SCENE 5

On stage: *For Michelle's Act:*
              Shimmery curtain
              Chair
              Club Lounge:
              As Act I, Scene 1

Furniture and Property List

SCENE 6

On stage: Kitchen units
Table. *On it:* bowl with bread dough, board, flour, recipe book, bread
    tin
Chairs
Ada's bag containing bottle of brown ale

SCENE 7

On stage: Pub setting

Off stage: Bag with snake (**Michelle**)
Bag (**Wendy**)

SCENE 8

On stage: *For Harry's speech:*
Nil
For Wendy's strip:
Gauze curtain
Chair
Wendy's robe

LIGHTING PLOT

Property fittings required: wall-brackets in club lounge, electric fire in Bernard's house, bedside lamp in bedroom
Several interior and one exterior settings

ACT I, Scene 1 Evening

To open: Spot on shimmery curtain

Cue 1	**Cilla** enters *Lighting on* **Cilla** *as she does her act*	(Page 1)
Cue 2	At end of **Cilla's** act *Black-out*	(Page 1)
Cue 3	When ready *Bring up interior lighting on club lounge—wall-brackets on*	(Page 1)
Cue 4	**Dougie:** " ... if that table's clear." (*They exit*) *Black-out*	(Page 6)

ACT I, Scene 2 Morning

To open: Interior lighting

Cue 5	**Buffy:** "... into a lifetime, doll." *Black-out*	(Page 11)

ACT I, Scene 3 Evening

To open: Interior lighting, electric fire on

Cue 6	**Wendy** gets out a business card *Black-out*	(Page 14)

ACT I, Scene 4 Day

To open: Interior lighting

Cue 7	**Harry:** "... go there on *Sunday*." *Black-out*	(Page 17)

ACT I, Scene 5 Morning

To open: Interior lighting

Cue 8	**Buffy:** "... then you're a stripper girl." *Black-out*	(Page 22)

ACT I, Scene 6 Evening

To open: Interior lighting, electric fire on

Cue 9	**Ada:** "Something always turns up—for the Robsons." *Black-out*	(Page 27)

ACT I, Scene 7 Evening

To open: Interior lighting

Cue 10   **Buffy:** "... with the stag audience ..."   (Page 27)
           Black-out

ACT I, Scene 8 Evening

To open: Spot on Harry

Cue 11   **Harry:** "... welcome to ... THE WONDERFUL
               WANDA ... "   (Page 29)
           Lighting on **Wendy** *as she does her strip*

ACT II, Scene 1 Day

To open: Interior lighting

Cue 12   **Ada:** "... when they are—watch out!"   (Page 33)
           Black-out

ACT II, Scene 2 Evening

To open: Exterior lighting

Cue 13   **Bernard** follows **Buffy** and **Dougie** off   (Page 34)
           Black-out

ACT II, Scene 3 Night

To open: Dim interior lighting

Cue 14   **Buffy** and **Dougie** enter   (Page 35)
           Bring up warm interior lighting

Cue 15   **Dougie** goes   (Page 38)
           Black-out

ACT II, Scene 4 Night

To open: Bedside lamp on

Cue 16   **Wendy:** "Should I put this book away?"   (Page 40)
           Black-out

ACT II, Scene 5 Evening

To open: Lighting on **Michelle** for strip

Cue 17   At end of **Michelle**'s strip   (Page 40)
           Black-out

Cue 18   When ready   (Page 40)
           Bring up interior lighting on club lounge—wall-brackets on

Cue 19	**Buffy:** "... in that suit ... whoo!"	(Page 43)
	Black-out	

ACT II, Scene 6 Evening

To open:	Interior lighting	
Cue 20	**Bernard** storms out	(Page 46)
	Black-out	

ACT II, Scene 7 Evening

To open:	Interior lighting	
No cues		

ACT II, Scene 8 Evening

To open:	Lighting on **Harry** in front of curtains	
Cue 21	Main tabs open	(Page 54)
	Lighting on **Wendy** *for strip*	

EFFECTS PLOT

ACT I

Cue 1	As Scene 1 opens *Voice-over of Club Secretary as per script*	(Page 1)
Cue 2	As **Cilla** enters and begins her act *Applause, then music for* **Cilla's** *strip, followed by applause*	(Page 1)
Cue 3	**Michelle:** "... guess from this?" (*She switches on tape recorder*) *Spurt of terrible discord*	(Page 18)
Cue 4	**Wendy:** "Shall I dance?" (*She switches on tape recorder*) *Music*	(Page 19)
Cue 5	**Wendy** switches off tape recorder *Snap off music*	(Page 19)
Cue 6	**Buffy:** "Next ..." (*Wendy switches on tape recorder*) *Different music—cut when* **Wendy** *switches off tape*	(Page 19)
Cue 7	**Wendy:** "...this might do." (*She switches on tape*) *Different music—cut as* **Wendy** *winds on tape*	(Page 19)
Cue 8	**Wendy:** "... this'll grab 'em ..." (*She switches on tape*) *Different music—cut when* **Wendy** *switches off tape*	(Page 19)
Cue 9	**Buffy** switches on tape recorder *Music—cut when* **Buffy** *switches off tape*	(Page 20)
Cue 10	**Buffy:** "... this grab you?" (*She switches on tape*) *Music: The Rolling Stones—cut when* **Buffy** *switches off tape*	(Page 20)
Cue 11	**Buffy:** "... to have a slow one." (*She switches on tape*) *Music—cut when* **Buffy** *switches off tape*	(Page 20)
Cue 12	**Michelle**'s tape recorder is switched on *Nautical music—cut at the end of* **Michelle's** *strip*	(Page 21)
Cue 13	**Harry:** "... THE WONDERFUL WANDA ..." *Applause, then music for* **Wendy's** *strip*	(Page 29)
Cue 14	**Paulie** chases **Bernard** and **Dougie** off stage *Cut music*	(Page 29)

ACT II

Cue 15	**Bernard:** "... behind my back." *Door slams, off*	(Page 31)
Cue 16	As Scene 5 opens *Music for* **Michelle's** *strip*	(Page 40)